"With a rare clarity of thought and a wealth of experience, Steve Blumenthal has given many of us invaluable advice on investing for more than twenty years. *On My Radar: Navigating Stock Market Cycles* is the text version of his extraordinary weekly On My Radar publication: chock full of insight, brilliant in its simplicity."

**—Wade Barnett, managing director, J.P. Morgan**

"Let others repeat how smart he is. I have known Steve for almost thirty years, and every minute spent has been my privilege. Next to my wife, he is my favorite breakfast partner."

**—Thomas D. Giachetti, Esq., chairman, Investment Management Practice Group**

"Steve Blumenthal's weekly On My Radar letter has been a must read for me for many years. *On My Radar: Navigating Stock Market Cycles* pulls together the best of Steve's thinking and provides you with a practical "how-to" guide that will help you navigate the challenges the coming restructuring of the sovereign debts and underfunded public pension systems will present. I call it the Great Reset. It will present, and we'll solve for it, but along the way will be periods of increased volatility. Steve suggests a sound process, a road map of sorts, for investors to know where they are in the market cycle, what that means in terms of probable future returns and relative risks, and how to both grow and defend your wealth."

**—John Mauldin**

"For forty years I have been doing investment research, and Steve is as thoughtful a mind as I have encountered during my career. He is disciplined and attacks all of his research with a 'prove it to me' attitude. He has never chased fads or overpriced markets. His thoughts are complete and come from a knowledge of investments that is deep. This book is based on all of that. He is clear and has developed a strategy that will allow anyone to pursue and reach their goals, while understanding there will be bumps on the way. We may be in for a decade of low returns because of today's high stock prices, but Steve's portfolios, thoughtfully designed to face this challenge, will thrive. If the 2030s are a decade of high returns, he will adjust his portfolios to take advantage of the opportunities the investment world presents at that time. Everyone needs a road map to reach their investment goals, and this is the Google Maps of investment portfolios."

**—Kevin Malone, Greenrock Research**

# ON MY RADAR
# NAVIGATING STOCK MARKET CYCLES

STEPHEN BLUMENTHAL

**ON MY RADAR**

# NAVIGATING STOCK MARKET CYCLES

## HOW TO GROW **AND** DEFEND YOUR WEALTH

ForbesBooks

Published by ForbesBooks, Charleston, South Carolina.
Member of Advantage Media Group.

ForbesBooks is a registered trademark, and the ForbesBooks colophon is a trademark of Forbes Media, LLC.

Printed in the United States of America.

10  9  8  7  6  5  4  3  2  1

ISBN: 978-1-946633-41-5
LCCN: 2020918563

Cover design by David Taylor.
Layout design by Megan Elger.

This custom publication is intended to provide accurate information and the opinions of the author in regard to the subject matter covered. It is sold with the understanding that the publisher, Advantage|ForbesBooks, is not engaged in rendering legal, financial, or professional services of any kind. If legal advice or other expert assistance is required, the reader is advised to seek the services of a competent professional.

Advantage Media Group is proud to be a part of the Tree Neutral® program. Tree Neutral offsets the number of trees consumed in the production and printing of this book by taking proactive steps such as planting trees in direct proportion to the number of trees used to print books. To learn more about Tree Neutral, please visit **www.treeneutral.com**.

Since 1917, Forbes has remained steadfast in its mission to serve as the defining voice of entrepreneurial capitalism. ForbesBooks, launched in 2016 through a partnership with Advantage Media Group, furthers that aim by helping business and thought leaders bring their stories, passion, and knowledge to the forefront in custom books. Opinions expressed by ForbesBooks authors are their own. To be considered for publication, please visit **www.forbesbooks.com**.

*To my beautiful wife, Susan, the love of my life. Endlessly grateful for you. And to our wonderful children, Brianna, Matthew, Kyle, Tyler, Connor, and Kieran. Thank you for the love and joy we share together! My sisters Amy and Sheryl and your families for your love and support. And you too Ashley Blumenthal.*

# CONTENTS

INTRODUCTION . . . . . . . . . . . . . . . . . . . . . . . . . 1

CHAPTER 1 . . . . . . . . . . . . . . . . . . . . . . 9
Cutting Through the Noise

CHAPTER 2 . . . . . . . . . . . . . . . . . . . . . . 29
How the Economic Machine Works

CHAPTER 3 . . . . . . . . . . . . . . . . . . . . . . 43
Short-Term Debt Cycles and Long-Term Debt Cycles

CHAPTER 4 . . . . . . . . . . . . . . . . . . . . . . 57
The Merciless Math of Loss

CHAPTER 5 . . . . . . . . . . . . . . . . . . . . . . 69
Recessions Matter

CHAPTER 6 . . . . . . . . . . . . . . . . . . . . . . 81
Balancing Offense vs. Defense

CHAPTER 7 . . . . . . . . . . . . . . . . . . . . . . 103
Where We Sit in the Economic and Market Cycles Matters

CHAPTER 8 . . . . . . . . . . . . . . . . . . . . . . .121

**Diversification Matters**

CHAPTER 9 . . . . . . . . . . . . . . . . . . . . . . 133

**Adapt to Succeed—How to Grow and Defend Your Wealth**

CHAPTER 10 . . . . . . . . . . . . . . . . . . . . . 149

**What Matters Most**

IMPORTANT DISCLOSURE INFORMATION. . . . . 173

DISCLOSURES. . . . . . . . . . . . . . . . . . . . . . 179

ACKNOWLEDGMENTS . . . . . . . . . . . . . . . . 183

ABOUT THE AUTHOR . . . . . . . . . . . . . . . . . 185

OUR SERVICES . . . . . . . . . . . . . . . . . . . . 187

## INTRODUCTION

I n the summer of 2018, major events in the United States and abroad captured our wide-eyed attention, perhaps none greater than the story of the Wild Boars, a youth soccer team in Thailand. The Wild Boars consisted of twelve boys age eleven to sixteen and their twenty-five-year-old coach. Here was a tale that gave us a chance to cheer for the team, to care, and to pray for a happy ending. Millions of people came together across the globe to share a powerful experience of concern for the well-being of these young men, hoping, together, for a positive outcome.

That fateful day started like any other. The team and coach were bicycling home after practice one day in late June and stopped by the Tham Luang cave system. Their plan was to celebrate a player's birthday and write their names on a cave wall, an initiation ritual they'd established on previous visits. An underground river flows through the cave. It was the beginning of monsoon season, and it started raining outside—hard. That rain unleashed flash floods that made the water inside rise ten feet within an hour.

The team was trapped. They could not go back the way they had come, fleeing deeper and farther into the cave until they came to a small rock ledge above the rushing, frigid water. Their perch was a mile underground and more than two miles from the cave entrance. Dwindling oxygen and lack of food and fresh water contributed to their growing concern. *Could they make it until someone found them? Would they even be found?*

Ten days after entering the cave, they were discovered alive. Holes were drilled from above to inject oxygen but missed the target. Seventeen days passed, oxygen levels worsened, and alternative escape routes were investigated.

For the rescuers, the rapidly changing logistics and conditions meant devising new tactics—sticking with the master plan but adjusting details as needed. How to get from here to there? The rescue team pieced together a plan that involved underwater oxygen tank stations, a pull-rope backup system, and many divers, each of them tethered to a child. It took several days to execute. A thirty-eight-year-old former Thai Navy Seal, Saman Gunan, who volunteered to help find the missing boys, died while placing air tanks along a proposed underwater escape route. In spite of this tragedy, the boys and their coach were pulled out alive one by one. Fitted with diving masks for underwater transit, the boys were given antianxiety medications, wrapped in space blankets, and strapped into flexible, wraparound stretchers. Mission impossible was achieved! I cheered—you cheered—and the world cheered.

Like those boys in the cave, our current global financial situation needs a solution in order to avoid crisis. We sit at the end of a long-term debt cycle. Few of us have seen one in our lifetimes, yet they have happened many times throughout history. At nearly $500 trillion in collective debt obligations (including unfunded US programs such as Social Security and Medicare) in a world producing $75 trillion, we find ourselves flooded in a sea of global debt that has reached a point where we require rescue.

We have made pension promises that are impossible to fulfill in their current form, and the timing of those payout obligations clashes with age demographics both in the United States and in most developed markets worldwide. For the baby boomers here in the United States, it's time to collect income from their pension plans, but in many places, the money to cover those payments is just not there. The likely solution is soon to be front-page news: lower payouts, higher taxes, or some form of government-sponsored bailout.

These deflationary pressures will slow the global economy. Ultimately, we will figure out how to monetize the debt and restructure the pension systems. There will be some form of global debt jubilee. On the path to the solution, there will be a number of violent storms. They will be as challenging as the 2008 Great Financial Crisis, yet different in form. To succeed financially, you'll need to know when the odds are stacked in your favor and when they are stacked against you. What matters most is having an understanding of where we sit in the market cycle and a game plan to navigate.

This book is about what matters and what you can do to successfully navigate the challenging times ahead. It's about growing and defending your wealth. It's about finding opportunity in calm waters and in crisis. It's about putting a game plan in place that successfully gets you and your wealth safely from here to the other side, no matter what those global conditions bring.

Whatever form the correction takes, when you create a disciplined investment process—one that seeks growth opportunities but also manages risk to minimize losses—you'll be able to take advantage of the environment, including the opportunities crises create. But it requires planning and preparing for the unexpected—much like what the Tham Luang rescue team did to bring those boys out of the cave. They held onto the rope and knew where the oxygen tanks were stashed.

Like most people, I was riveted by the Wild Boars' misadventure and its aftermath, especially since I had been a soccer player and coach myself. The team, rescuers, and helpers were inspirational; the lessons and takeaways were illuminating.

As soon as the boys' bicycles and soccer cleats were discovered outside the cave, rescuers began strategizing to launch what felt like an impossible mission. Some thought the rescue was too dangerous, the chances of success too small to warrant the risk. The cave system had never been fully mapped, and they didn't know the boys' location. There was darkness, limited oxygen, strong currents, and flood waters cold enough to cause hypothermia to contend with. If by some miracle they were still alive, the soccer team was at tremendous risk—and the responders would be too.

Ten days into the ordeal, with hope fading fast, two British divers discovered the team on the ledge, almost by happenstance. In another turn of good luck, a fourteen-year-old spoke English and was able to translate. Finding all thirteen players alive was exhilarating, but the difficulties were just beginning. Most of the boys couldn't swim, and the exit route was long, with much of it underwater. The team had already gone a long time without food before being found. They were weak and skeletally thin. Some suggested they might have to remain in the cave for four months, until the end of monsoon season.

How did they survive? Turns out the assistant coach, known as Coach Ek, had been orphaned as a young boy and had entered a Buddhist monastery, where he'd lived as a novice for more than a decade. Now, as the lone adult in charge of the team, he taught them a skill he knew well: meditation. It calms the emotions and slows the metabolism and breathing, thereby reducing the body's resource consumption. Coach Ek's decision to share that skill may have saved the boys' lives.

I won't pretend that investment management carries the same kind of consequences as this incredible rescue endeavor. But it's a pretty good bet that if you succumb to fear, denial, anger, defeatism, or panic—all common responses when the market takes a turn—you'll have a harder time getting through the challenging investment landscape ahead. Why? Because strong emotions impede clear thinking. They can quickly sweep your logic and reason away like the current of a flash flood.

The ability to set your emotions aside for the moment will be extremely beneficial in distinguishing what really matters from what doesn't as you create and execute your investing strategy—an approach controlled in process and absent of emotion. Working with an unclouded mind helps you assess more accurately what your current situation is, which is essential in figuring out how to build the bridge that will get you or—if you are an investment advisor—your clients successfully to the other side of the turbulent period we face ahead.

> It's a pretty good bet that if you succumb to fear, denial, anger, defeatism, or panic—all common responses when the market takes a turn—you'll have a harder time getting through the challenging investment landscape ahead.

I've been honing this kind of mental discipline and discernment skill in the financial industry for more than thirty-five years. Fresh out of Penn State, accounting degree in hand, I landed my first investment job on an option arbitrage desk at Merrill Lynch. That was in 1984. I spent a year on the institutional side of the business and then became a financial consultant working with individual investors. That proved to be a valuable education for me. I remember how fear overcame reason en masse during the October 1987 stock market crash. My mentor, John Ray, a senior portfolio manager at a major mutual fund company, later told me he saw the fear factor in play among many of the professional portfolio managers at his firm as well.

Two years before the crash, John had handed me his copy of *Reminiscences of a Stock Operator* by Edwin LeFevre, telling me it was the most important financial book I'd ever read. First published in 1923, *Reminiscences* is a fictionalized account of the life of the securities trader Jesse Livermore. It offers insights into the art of trading and speculation. John looked me in the eyes and said, "I want it back."

After the '87 market crash, John quizzed me on the book. He said, "Investing is emotional, and that is one constant that will never change." His message to me was that what happened in the 1920s and 1930s would happen repeatedly over the balance of my career. "Make sure you factor that into your thinking," he said. I've witnessed this firsthand in the years since then, many times over: fear and greed spur investors to act erratically and irrationally. It causes them to focus on an abundance of economic myths and misconceptions—much to their detriment.

What I learned from John was more than a career lesson; it was an awakening. I've seen so many people make costly mistakes—mistakes that could have been avoided with proper planning, a disciplined process, and an honest self-awareness that allows them to see opportunity when the majority of investors see a crisis.

Several years after reading *Reminiscences*, I met the great investor and philanthropist Sir John Templeton at a lunch at the Union League in downtown Philadelphia. In a room full of other brokers and consultants, Sir John shared what he said was the greatest piece of advice he had to give: "The secret to my success is that I buy when everyone else is selling and I sell when everyone else is buying." Sage advice. These moments present again and again over time.

In 1992, I founded CMG Capital Management Group, where I serve as executive chairman and chief investment officer. CMG works with a select team of independent investment advisors, individuals, and institutions. We incorporate best-in-class investment and risk-management strategies and provide access to select investment opportunities to create and safeguard wealth. Augmented by partnerships with world-renowned thought leaders and investment managers, CMG's innovative strategies and financial instruments are aimed at increasing portfolio stability with the objective of pursuing growth opportunities while maintaining an important level of risk protection in down markets.

The tactics change depending on your circumstances. If you are twenty-five years old, simply dollar-cost average into the stock market each year and know you'll have several significant bear market correction opportunities to double down when prices are low and opportunities are great. However, if you are a preretiree or a retiree like me, you may not have the time to recover. It can take ten or fifteen years with inflation factored in just to get back to even. Unfortunately, preretirees and retirees just don't have that kind of time. Still, it can be hard to stay rational and realistic about that reality— and many others.

In most cases, investors and financial professionals just stampede with the herd. I believe it's largely because they don't understand the economic forces at work and the emotional tendencies that influence our complex financial system. But when you know better, you can do better. I've written this book to help increase the visibility of what matters and encourage you to create an investment game plan that is risk minded and enables you to be cautious when others are greedy and see opportunity when others see fear. We sit at the end of a long-term debt accumulation cycle. My dear friend and business partner John Mauldin calls what lies immediately ahead "The Great Reset," a restructuring of the global debt and underfunded pension liabilities. The challenges such periods present are substantial. You can certainly navigate these risks successfully, but you'll need an investment game plan in place to make it through. That's what we'll do here.

I'll tell you about methods for cutting through the distracting and meaningless noise in order to focus on the issues that really matter and determine what to do next.

To give you a better grounding in investment management, we'll lift the hood to see the basic principles that run the economic engine, including debt cycles and recessions. Then we'll take a deep breath and discuss the sobering truth about loss and why minimizing losses—conserving those resources when the oxygen gets low—is far more important than beating the market in any given year.

Up or down, wherever markets are perched when you're reading this, you'll learn how to create simple strategies and choose investment solutions that best serve your needs or those of your clients—in both good times and bad. We'll talk about investment efficiency, balancing offense and defense, and how to use tactical trend-following methods to seek growth opportunities and avoid significant losses. And we'll explore an approach to wealth management and portfolio construction that is holistic and comprehensive, yet simple and direct.

It's natural to want financial abundance in our lives. And I'm optimistic about our ability to achieve and maintain it. Economics and investing are often made more complicated than they need to be. I hope *On My Radar: Navigating Stock Market Cycles* helps you focus in on what counts and create a disciplined process to grow and defend your wealth, regardless of what's happening on a global scale.

# CHAPTER 1

# Cutting Through the Noise

E very day, we're bombarded with new information. Today's news—whether in the form of trade deals or tweets—tips the market in one direction or another, but the question is, Does it matter? Often, the answer is no: most of it is designed to grab our attention in order to increase advertising revenues. The latest bulletin may send the market up or down, but generally those moves quickly fade away. In the end, unless you are a high-frequency day trader, my best advice is to tune it out. It is unimportant, it doesn't matter, and it often distracts us from the stuff that matters.

To understand how this plays out, let's flash back to 2007. Everyone is bullish, with what they feel is good reason: the housing market is booming, the stock market is strong, consumer confidence is soaring, and by virtually every measure the economy looks solid. But it isn't. Rather, it is propped up on a massive supply of subprime mortgage debt, and that—along with a host of other factors—is about to nearly bring down the entire financial house.

The stock market peaked in October 2007, and a year later, the

Great Financial Crisis took hold. In October of 2007, the noise was telling investors that everything was okay, but what mattered—and what the majority of people didn't see—was the fragile state of the system.

When I got a call in 2006 from one of the smartest investors I know, my friend Mark Finn, I knew something was up. "Steve, check your portfolio. Do any of the managers have subprime, mortgage-backed securities, CDO exposure?"

"What are you seeing, Mark?" I asked.

CDOs, collateralized debt obligations, are a Wall Street–invented product. A collection of pooled assets (like subprime mortgages) neatly delivered in various tranches you could buy, depending on your risk appetite. Squash together a bunch of no-doc, no-down payment, high-risk mortgages, send it to Moody's for a AAA stamp of approval, and sell those yield-hungry unsuspecting investors the highly rated, high-yielding debt they're looking for.

When you're deep inside the capital markets machine and regularly speak with smart people, you see things. Mark and his team get pitched on just about everything. One of those pitches was from a manager betting big time against those garbage mortgage pools. Then another made the same pitch. Lights on.

The subprime housing crisis is well documented in Michael Lewis's book *The Big Short*. Back then, it was on very few people's radars, but it was on ours. There was nothing about it in the mainstream news. Frankly, it was just the opposite. According to the masses, everything was rosy. But the combination of low interest rates and investors' desire for higher-yielding bonds led the creative bankers on Wall Street to manufacture new AAA-rated paper that was simply a bundle of no-doc mortgages issued to the least creditworthy of borrowers. All that extra liquidity found its way into the housing markets, and the economy looked awesome—until it became clear that it was just a house of cards.

I began writing about the layers and layers of Wall Street–created leveraged mortgage products and how junk mortgages packed into CDOs could receive a AAA rating, though they were really the worst of the bad mortgages. Few wanted to hear such news, yet the enormity of the risk was in plain sight if you looked.

In mid-2007, a Bear Stearns hedge fund cracked. *There it is,* I said to myself. *That matters!* Alan Greenspan assured the public that the economy was in good shape, adding that the housing market had never had a major correction. But his low-interest policy enabled a lot of bad behavior, like subprime mortgages, and within a year the world's greatest financial system was brought to its knees. The signals were there: a low, continuous siren, but the noise—all the stuff that didn't matter—was drowning it out.

That brings us to a key insight: Equity markets and economies cycle above and below relatively predictable long-term growth trends. Where we sit at any particular time in these cycles matters. Investment conditions are best at the market bottoms and worst at the market tops. This is measurable and easy to see. Are we above the long-term growth trend or below it? How much are we paying for the assets we are buying? Valuation levels tell us a great deal about coming returns three, five, seven, ten, and twelve years from now. The Fed matters. Fiscal policy matters. The magnitude of debt matters. High levels of debt impede growth. Where are we in the debt cycle? Where are interest rates? How do they compare to others around the globe? Where are we in the business cycle? Recessions matter. What are recession-watch indicators signaling (it is in recessions that the really bad bear markets occur)? Demographics matter. All of this can inform and shape your investment positioning. All of this matters.

Answering those questions would have helped investors see what was brewing in 1999 and 2007. But most investors weren't asking them in the first place.

For those of us tasked with managing money and coaching and guiding others, there are times to play defense and times to play offense. Take an adaptive investment approach—more defense than offense—when cycles are aged and overvalued, and play more offense than defense when asset valuations and forward returns are best. Emotionally, this is hard for many investors to comprehend, for in the moment the opposite feels true. I speak with experience—from my early days working for Merrill Lynch in the 1980s to today—when I say the majority of investors behave badly and do the wrong things at the wrong times. If you are tuned in to what matters, you'll be better prepared to take advantage of their misbehavior.

Let's look at this another way. Maybe you're like me and you love to ski. If you do, you know there's nothing like the excitement of a winter storm. The feeling you get when you softly float down a mountain in two feet of fresh powder is one of the great natural highs. Now, picture storm after storm. Multiple layers of snow build up. Between storms, the sun may warm the surface before the next freeze, forming a crust. Storm after storm, layer upon layer—what develops is an unstable environment. Risk of avalanche is high. The fresh snowfall looks beautiful, but underneath the surface lies risk. That's what happens at market tops. We don't know exactly which event or piece of news will cause the slide. In March 2007, it was a Bear Stearns subprime hedge fund that tripped the avalanche that is now known as the Great Financial Crisis.

Over time, systems move from periods of stability to instability, from low risk to high risk and from high risk back to low and with calm periods in between. Investors will always find a reason to keep skiing. That new snow is great news, but what matters most are the layers of instability beneath it.

The market won't correct when we want it to or when we believe it will happen. Nobody knows the particular event that is going to trip the avalanche. What we do know is that the snow is unstable— that matters. Fortunately, we can measure where we sit in an investment cycle, and we can accurately zero in on what that tells us about future returns. And we can adapt our approach to the conditions presented to us. It's up to you to know if the powder is resting on layers of thin ice and when it is safe to let your skis run.

> The market won't correct when we want it to or when we believe it will happen. Nobody knows the particular event that is going to trip the avalanche. What we do know is that the snow is unstable.

## Drowning Out What Doesn't Matter

*What the wise man does in the beginning,*
*the fool does in the end.*
**—Warren Buffett**

Investing is often a game of opposites. The great Sir John Templeton said the secret of his success is that he buys when everyone is selling and sells when everyone is buying. But instead, people often believe that confidence is a sign that things will continue to head upward. However, throughout history, when confidence has been high, the subsequent performance in the stock market has been low.

It's very counterintuitive, but the logic is pretty simple. When confidence is high, people are fully invested, they're all in; they've largely committed their money to equities. And fully invested means there is less money available to buy stocks. More buyers than sellers pushes prices up. More sellers than buyers drives prices down. In Sir John's day, it was more about feel than hard data. Today, we have the data at our fingertips. Investors would be better off following Sir John's great advice. Unfortunately for the majority of investors, they tend to buy and sell at the wrong times—honestly, do you know anyone who was buying stocks in 2009?

To put this into perspective, we can see investor misbehavior in the data. Just prior to the great tech crash, investor money-market assets represented 10 percent of the total market value of the US stock market. Only once since 1980 were money-market balances that low. The lowest on record was 9.31 percent, just prior to the October 1987 crash. A year before the 2007 market top, money-market balances relative to the total market value was a low 12.74 percent. It was a measurable "sell when everyone is buying" moment.

The reverse is true at market bottoms. Panic selling took money-market balances to 23.97 percent near the equity market bottom in 2003 and to a record 46.91 percent at the equity market low in 2009. Ned Davis Research found four periods of ultrahigh money-market asset balances: 23.71 percent in 1982, 19.62 percent in 1990, 23.97 percent in 2003, and 46.91 percent in 2009. They found four periods of ultralow market balances: 9.31 percent in 1987, 10.01 percent in 1998, 12.74 percent in 2006 and 9.06 percent in 2018.[1]

The bottom line: There is a high correlation between money-market balances and subsequent annual equity market returns. Returns are highest when money-market balances are high, and returns are lowest when market balances are low. When you hear the popular media outlets espousing optimistic news, think more like

---

1    Ned Davis Research.

Sir John and less like the average Joe. Put the daily media noise in the "doesn't matter" category. The wise man buys when confidence is low. The fools come in at the end.

With so much noise flooding our senses and newsfeeds today, how do we avoid the herd mentality and get to the heart of the, well, matter? How can we mark our calendars for avalanche season, even if we can't pinpoint the exact storm that will bring it on?

## Identifying What Matters

*In the absence of the ability to see the future, how can we position our portfolios for what lies ahead? Much of the answer lies in understanding where the market stands in its cycle and what that implies for its future movements.*
### —Howard Marks

When it comes to predicting the future, there are many ways to go about it. The Fed has a thousand PhDs on staff running models to try to predict what will and won't happen. Some investors fall into the camp of the late John Bogle of Vanguard, who believed that nobody can really figure out this stuff, and the only way to proceed is to buy and hold on tight—putting 60 percent of your money in the stock market and the other 40 percent into the bond market, and rebalancing every year.

Others believe they have a strong ability to look at companies, read their balance sheets, and determine the very best investments to make from that information. Some, like Paul Tudor Jones, believe they can trade the trend movements in the market and profit. Others, like Howard Marks, believe where the market stands in its cycle and what that implies for its future movements matters. But the bottom line is that all of them have an investment process, and what matters most is that they stick to it—that's the key to their success.

Before we get into the ins and outs of shaping your own invest-ment process, let's take a look at some of the things that *matter*.

## Debt Cycles Matter

Put understanding debt, short- and long-term debt cycles, and where we are within those cycles in the *matters* category. We can tap the brilliant investor, hedge-fund manager, and philanthropist Ray Dalio for a deeper understanding of how the economy, debt, and debt cycles work—and why they're so crucial. We'll discuss this in greater detail in Chapters 2 and 3, but here's the gist of his framework, as explained to Mike McKee and Tom Keene during a 2017 Bloomberg Surveillance interview:

It's our productivity that produces income. At the end of the day, you can spend what you earn, and what you earn is a function of your productivity—determined by both hard work and creativ-ity. This is true for individuals and larger entities like businesses and countries. Meanwhile, credit (which turns to debt as soon as it's granted) is a multiplier. It enables you to spend more than you earn. The borrowing, spending, and growth made possible by credit is good for the economy, sending it skyward. But a point is reached when you have to pay back what you previously borrowed. This dynamic creates cycles—both short- and long-term.

We're used to the short-term, or business, cycle. In this one, people borrow and spend freely. But at a certain point, monetary policy tightens, and the Fed raises interest rates. Some people can no longer afford to cover their debts. Recessions happen, and the Fed eases, reducing interest rates. As a result, asset prices go up and borrowing costs go down. Inflation happens. Policies tighten again to manage it, and the economy starts to go down. Every economy is somewhere in that cycle.

These business cycles add up over time, creating long-term debt cycles. What do these look like? Say you're starting off your career without any debt. You earn $100,000. Then you borrow $10,000, giving you the opportunity to spend $110,000. Your spending is someone else's income. In turn, they earn more, allowing them to spend more too. It becomes self-reinforcing until you reach the point where debts are too high relative to income (like a balance sheet, at some point you can't borrow any more money because you owe too much relative to what you earn). At that point, something must be done to relieve the debt burden.

All central banks are in the business of helping this process along. They lower interest rates, and then lower them again until they hit 0 percent. Now, we come to a dilemma: We reach the end of traditional monetary policy, and as a result, we can't keep that long-term cycle going. At this point, the central banks can't create credit, because there's already too much debt, so they print money and put it into the system by buying financial assets. When they buy bonds, the seller takes that cash and purchases something else. That causes longer-term yields to fall as the buying drives asset prices up. There are three equilibria here:

1. Debts can't rise faster than income for long.

2. The operating rate in the economy can't be too loose or too tight.

3. Regarding the capital markets structure, cash is going to have a lower yield than bonds, which is going to have a lower return than equities, and so on.

As of this writing, the United States is in the middle of a short-term debt cycle. We're also nearing or at the end of a long-term debt cycle. Since monetary and fiscal policy are the tools we use to work through short-term and long-term debt cycles, we also have to ask what the Fed will do about our current position and why (as you've likely guessed, this matters too).

## What the Fed Will Do and Why It Matters

Put simply, the Fed matters because it controls interest rates. When interest rates go up, it affects where people invest their money and how it flows globally. For example, we've had thirteen increasing interest rate cycles since 1950, where the Fed tried to slow the economy and prevent inflation by raising interest rates. Ten of them ended in recessions.

The Fed's goal is to keep employment strong and prices stable. To determine their course of action, the Fed is heavily reliant on—if not married to—a limited equation called the Phillips Curve. Named after William Phillips, it's a single-equation empirical model that describes a historical inverse relationship between rates of unemployment and inflation within an economy. It assumes that high levels of employment will pressure wages, increase incomes and spending, and drive inflation higher. That's true in short-term debt (or business) cycles, but is it always true? In my view, the answer is no. As such, the Phillips Curve doesn't see the long-term debt cycle.

Still, because how the Fed will likely react falls into the *matters* category, the Phillips Curve does, too, since it's what the Fed is focused on. How we reset the debt via a combination of monetary and fiscal policy will dictate what Ray Dalio refers to as a "beautiful" or "ugly" outcome.

What does he think will happen? Ray believes the central banks will be pressured to ease monetary policy (lower rates) versus tightening (raising rates) it. He explained, "We are in an asymmetrical world where the risk of raising rates is far greater than lowering rates."[2]

He's saying we can't have a big rate rise because of the amount of debt out there because of what it will do to the dollar and because of the disinflation it would cause, leading to a downturn. Instead, he thinks the next big Fed move will be to provide more quantitative easing (QE). QE creates money out of thin air, and the central banks use that money to buy assets from you and me. Then we have money in our accounts that we can put to work. But unfortunately, QE won't work as well as it did last time—each time, it's just less effective.[3]

## Market Valuations and Probable Seven-, Ten-, and Twelve-Year Returns Matter

Valuations matter too. They can tell us little about timing tops and bottoms, but they can tell us a great deal about coming seven-, ten-, and twelve-year returns and alert us to periods of heightened risk.

We had the Nifty Fifty stocks craze in the 1970s, Portfolio Insurance in the mid-1980s, Tech in the 1990s, and Real Estate in the mid-2000s (that easy mortgage capital creatively engineered on Wall Street—slices and dices of subprime junk somehow sleeved into AAA-rated tranches that enabled massive amounts of mortgage liquidity). Who would have imagined they would nearly collapse the global financial system?

What remained relatively consistent in all the prior periods was the relationship between equity market valuations and the subsequent ten-year return outcomes. What is also true is that on the other side of those bubbles was a great investment opportunity.

---

2    Ray Dalio, "Financial Crisis 2017 The Economic Reality Ray Dalio Interview," YouTube video, posted July 20, 2017, https://www.youtube.com/watch?v=z9K6W hPUyUI&feature=youtu.be.

3    Ibid.

The data can tell us a great deal about probable coming returns and levels of risk. Since it's easy to get caught up in a world of financial terminology, I'm going to try my best to explain valuations in a way that my wife, Susan—who is very passionate about coaching soccer and less so about investing—or an individual client might better understand, starting with price-to-earnings ratio, or P/E.

Susan has a soccer coaching business. If she earned $50,000 (a made-up number) and her company had 50,000 shares outstanding, her company earned $1 per share. Keep that in mind as a data point. Now, if I could invest in her business by purchasing her stock at a price of $24 per share, how would I know if I'm getting a good deal or a bad one? I want to make as high a return as I can. The price means nothing if I don't consider how much money her company can earn.

You can look at the price of Susan's stock ($24) relative to her company's earnings ($1) and determine if you are getting a lot for your money (high future return on investment) or a little for your money (low return).

If her company earns $1 and is trading at $24, then her price relative to her earnings had a P/E ratio of 24. Consider that to be your second data point. You can compare that number to other points in time and see if you are getting a bargain or paying too much.

Of course, her business might hit a home run in regards to earnings next year, but if we think of the overall stock market in general, companies collectively grow their earnings by about as much as the United States grows its economy each year (about 2 percent per year since January 2000). We can also factor in things like debt levels, tax cuts, interest rates, and global growth to see if that earnings number can pick up, but let's keep it simple for now. We don't need all those other factors because current actual reported P/E levels tell us most of what we need to know about future returns.

Now, if Susan's stock price were $17 per share, her company would be trading at a P/E of seventeen times that $1 of earnings. If her stock were at $10, her company would be trading at a P/E of ten times earnings. That'd be a steal so long as she could maintain her earnings. Can you see how what you pay relative to what a company can earn can help you determine the good or bad future return you might receive?

Let's see what happens when we look at the broad stock market. Since many people consider the stock market to be the S&P 500 Index, we'll use that as a proxy. The S&P 500 Index is a collection of the largest US companies, but think of it as one large company you can buy. Looking at data back to 1964, the median price-to-earnings ratio was 17.2. Think of that level as fair value. In November 2019, Median P/E was 23.8. We can look over a long data set and get a feel for just how high or low a price might be relative to its long-term fair value. To put 23.8 into perspective, Median P/E reached a high of 28 in late 1999 and 26.8 in January 2018. Prior to 1999, it had never been higher than 22.6. It was at 12.2 in November 2008. So, 23.8 is a high number.

Again, think of that as a data point. If Susan earned $1 per share and the price of her stock was $23.80 per share, her current P/E ratio would be 23.80. If you buy her stock, you are paying a rich price. Better to buy it when the market corrects to fair valve or lower. A much better entry point would be $17.20.

This is where the historical data becomes important. If we took all the month-end Median P/E readings and sorted them into five groups (quintiles), ranging from the lowest P/Es to the highest P/Es, and then calculated the actual ten-year annualized returns that followed, we would see that what we pay for an asset relative to its prior twelve-month actual earnings really matters. If Susan's stock P/E was 10, we'd be in quintile 1 with expectations to gain 15.7 percent annually over the coming ten years. Would you rather buy at a P/E of 23.80 (quintile 5) with a probable return forecast of 4.3 percent or a P/E of 10 with a probable return forecast of 15.7 percent? The best returns are when your investment starting condition is in the lowest quintile and your worst returns are when your investment starting condition is in the highest, or most expensive, quintile.

Here is a look at the data (1926 to December 31, 2014):

| RETURNS BY P/E QUINTILE | |
|---|---|
| P/E Ratio Quintile<br>(1 = Lowest, 5 = Highest) | Return<br>(Median Annualized Total<br>Return Subsequent 10 Years) |
| 1 | 15.7% |
| 2 | 12.9% |
| 3 | 9.9% |
| 4 | 7.8% |
| 5 | 4.3% |

Bottom line: We sit in quintile 5 at the time of this writing. The stock market is richly priced; expect forward returns to be low. Put valuations in the *matters* column.

There are a number of measures that can tell us how the market is priced. None of them can tell us when the market might turn. But those numbers *do* tell us what the probable returns are likely to be over the next ten years. When the market is exceptionally priced, we can zero in on a range of what the returns are likely to be over the coming seven, ten, and twelve years. If evidence shows that prices are high relative to earnings, statistically, future returns will be low. We'll look at this in more detail in Chapter 6, Balancing Offense vs. Defense.

## Price Matters

In addition to valuations, price matters. Here's a quick anecdote from the great American investor, hedge-fund manager, and philanthropist Paul Tudor Jones that highlights why. Paul taught an undergraduate class at the University of Virginia. He told his students he could provide them with a single insight that would save them the cost of an MBA. All they had to do was put a two-hundred-day stop-loss moving average on everything they owned. Why?

Paul said, "I've seen too many things go to zero, stocks and commodities. The whole trick to investing is 'How do I keep from losing everything?' If you use the two-hundred-day moving average rule, then you get out. You play defense, and you get out."[4]

What he's saying—and I wholeheartedly agree—is to focus in on what price behavior is telling you. Why? Because in a free market, everything meets at the point of price—every buyer, every seller. No matter what you think, what somebody else thinks, or what the latest news is saying, look at what's happening to price.

You've heard the phrase, "the trend is your friend." That's what Paul is saying, and he uses the two-hundred-day moving average price to measure the intermediate-term trend of what he owns. He selects an investment for a particular reason, and when it's above the two-hundred-day price trend line he stays in. The process serves as confirmation that his decision to hold onto that asset is correct. But if the price drops below its two-hundred-day moving-average-price trend line, he gets out. While he has perfectly sound fundamental reasoning for believing his investment will advance, he is balanced enough to know he is not always right. The trend in price matters. We'll look at several ways price can help you better manage risk in Chapter 6.

---

4   "Paul Tudor Jones: Top Market Wizard and Trend Trader," Turtletrader.com, accessed January 13, 2019, https://www.turtletrader.com/trader-jones/.

## Investment Process Matters

This brings us to process. I know not everyone wants to get into the weeds of the market. Many people think about this stuff similarly to the way I do about the electrical system in my home. I recently encountered a problem, and with the knowledge that taking things into my own hands would be a dangerous proposition no matter how many how-to videos I watched online, I called my electrician. He fixed the problem, and then he attempted to show me exactly what he had done. "Listen," I told him, "I certainly don't want to be rude, but I just don't care as long as it works." There's a process-driven route for you, whether you want to get deep in the weeds or you just want it to work. Finding the right process (even if that means hiring a professional who can implement one for you) can help anyone— no matter how advanced or interested—navigate the information they need and tune out the stuff that doesn't matter, including a big downfall for many investors: emotion. Process takes emotion out of the equation.

We know that markets cycle over periods of time; thus, there are periods when it makes sense to play more offense than defense and periods when it makes sense to play more defense than offense.

Since 1900, there have been five secular, or long-term, bull markets and four secular bear markets. During secular bull periods, the annual gain for the S&P 500 index averaged 13.7 percent. And those five bull markets occurred approximately 55 percent of the time. During secular bear markets, the S&P 500 index lost 4 percent per year on average. Secular bear markets occurred approximately 45 percent of the time. The key point here is that markets cycle from bull to bear to bull again.

If you put an investment game plan in place that considers where we sit in the economic cycle, where we may sit in the equity market cycle, and the level of equity market valuations and what they tell us about probable forward returns while incorporating a disciplined downside-risk-management game plan, you'll do just fine over time. You're going to avoid the major market crashes and be in a position to take advantage of the opportunities they create. Looking back at the returns by quintile data, there is a major data point that's not evident: not only do you achieve the highest returns when your starting conditions are in quintile 1, that's also when your risk level is lowest. However, the reverse is true when you are in quintiles 4 and 5. Returns are lowest and risk is highest.

Risk and reward can be measured and managed. High complacency and good news are seen at market tops. Panic, volatility, and a high correlation are seen at market bottoms. Your best opportunities will present when you feel fear the most. Your worst opportunities arrive when you are overconfident and complacent. If you stick to your process, it will be that much easier to block the noise out.

Successful investors have a process for selecting investments and managing risk. That's part of what we'll do here. By the time you're done reading this book, you'll have tools to help you understand where we are in the economic and equity market cycles, how to avoid and profit from recessions, what valuations tell you about coming returns, and how a simple, disciplined process can help you know when to play more defense and when to play more offense. And we'll look at ways you can manage your risk exposures, enabling you to systematically grow and defend your wealth.

## The Future is Worse Than You Think

As I write this book in 2019, the indicators are pointing to challenging financial times beginning within the next year or two. The US equity bull market is the longest in history. The US business cycle is in the longest expansion in history. And the most concerning issue of our day is that we sit at the end of a long-term debt super cycle. The last long-term debt cycle peaked in the mid-1930s. Few of us have seen one. Most are unaware of the magnitude of the problem. Risks are elevated due to interest rates at near record-low yields and valuations sitting at the second highest level in history—higher than 1929, 1966, 1987, and 2007. Only the top of the great dotcom technology bubble in 2000 was higher. How much lifespan remains on the upswing is yet to be seen.

The message is clear: we are nearing what economist, author, and strategist Dr. Mohamed El-Erian calls a "T Juncture." We're coming to the end of a road where we must turn left or right, because continuing straight, the way we've been traveling, is no longer an option. The global central bankers are attempting to end years of QE, with more than $16 trillion in collective asset purchases. Liquidity that was created out of thin air and injected into global markets successfully inflated asset prices.

Further, zero-bound interest-rate policy has sent investors into riskier asset classes, encouraged corporations to borrow and buy back their own stocks, and enabled an unknown number of "zombie companies" to live and survive on debt. At the same time, ultralow yields have taken a huge toll on pension plans, insurance companies, and retiree returns. Pension plans in particular have missed their return bogeys (benchmarks) and sit massively underfunded, with a surge of retirees ready to start collecting. We are nearing a tipping point—a complex problem that will require a solution. How will we get from here to there?

My friend and colleague John Mauldin uses the term "The Great Reset" to describe the big picture of the coming economic downturn.

It will be caused by what he says are the two largest bubbles ever experienced. One is debt that far outstrips productivity, much of it government debt. The second is what he calls government promises, that is, unfunded or underfunded pensions. The pension problem is fueled by demographics in the United States, where members of the enormous baby boom generation (born between 1946 and 1964) are at or nearing retirement age.

The potential negatives are mounting. A recession or two that bring market declines of 50 to 70 percent is in the realm of possibility. These are not doom-and-gloom predictions intended to scare you. Rather, they're informed assessments based on economic principles that have borne out many times over hundreds of years.

The good news: by paying attention to what matters—and implementing a strong investment process—you can position and manage your wealth in a way that will get you from here to there. It's important to be mindful, too, that the next crisis—like crises past—will create outstanding investment opportunities. You'll want to get to that opportunity. We'll talk about how, but let's first take a look into the framework for it all: how the economic machine works.

# CHAPTER 2

# How the Economic Machine Works

I f you knew you had an advancing medical issue and you could do something about it to avoid extreme damage, would you? For most of us, the answer is a resounding yes. But how do you know you have a problem if you and your doctor don't know what to look for? Put simply, you can't. You're more likely to overlook serious symptoms and react too slowly—compromising good outcomes in the process.

But when you know what matters, the prognosis changes. You can be proactive and tackle your health issues head-on, with the confidence that early detection and swift action will help you ride the wave of your illness and make it through to the other side. Think of this chapter as an economic physical of sorts—one where you'll come to understand how the economic corpus works, laying the groundwork for successful diagnosis and treatment.

To do that effectively, we first need to find the right practitioner. While it can be interesting to hear a variety of perspectives, I must say, I don't weigh them all equally (it *is* our health we're talking about, after all—financial or otherwise). A young CFA comes to mind. He has strong convictions, no proven history, and very little self-awareness. With too few hits from the school of hard knocks and way too much bravado, I give little weight to what he has to say. Put his two cents in the *doesn't matter* column.

On the other side of the spectrum is someone like Ray Dalio. If you're not familiar with Dalio, one of the greatest investors of all time, consider this your primer. His firm, Bridgewater Associates, is the world's largest hedge fund. They are agnostic to direction. They bet up. They bet down. Success depends on being on the right side of the trade. And they're good—so good that they manage $160 billion and clients pay a fee of 2 percent and 20 percent of profits for their services. According to an interview on *60 Minutes*, Bridgewater has produced profitable results for its clients in twenty-five of the last twenty-eight years.[5] Dalio's two cents fall squarely in the *matters* column.

He chalks up his ability to avoid the perils of the 2008 financial crisis to a template he and his team created—one that can be universally applied to all debt crises. And he's made that information public, sharing his insights in his book *Principles for Navigating Big Debt Crises*, which is available for free on the Bridgewater web site. It is a master class on how economies work, how they cycle, how bubbles begin, how they end, who wins, who loses, and how you and I might better navigate the future. Dalio has also created an easy-to-understand video, "How the Economic Machine Works," which breaks his theories down to their most basic components. You can—and should—watch it at https://www.economicprinciples. org/. When you're done, send it to your children.

---

5    Bill Whitaker, "Ray Dalio Says Wealth Inequality Is a National Emergency," CBSNews.com, July 28, 2019, https://www.cbsnews.com/news/ray-dalio-capitalism-needs-reform-wealth-inequality-is-a-national-emergency-60-min-utes-2019-07-28/.

Why is he sharing his work so readily? Frankly, to do good. His mission is to help people—including policy makers—understand how the economic machine works; how debt drives business cycles; and how, over many years, debt accumulates to a point where something must happen—what John Mauldin has deemed "The Great Reset." Dalio's hope is that those in control will be more informed and act accordingly. The decisions made by global central bankers and policy makers will determine just how bumpy the future will be. The outcome ranges from what Dalio calls "beautiful" to "ugly." In his April 2019 *60 Minutes* interview, Dalio put the probability for a beautiful outcome at 35 percent and an ugly outcome at 65 percent.[6] With his help, we have the potential to make it through with the least amount of pain—and take advantage of significant opportunities—but we've got to listen up.

> The outcome ranges from what Dalio calls "beautiful" to "ugly." In his April 2019 *60 Minutes* interview, Dalio put the probability for a beautiful outcome at 35 percent and an ugly outcome at 65 percent.

In the next two chapters, we'll cover some of the content captured in both of Dalio's pieces to build a better understanding of the economic system, including the forces that will lead to the next big downturn. So grab a coffee, find your favorite chair, and settle in. It's time for Dalio's lesson on the economic anatomy and what it can tell us about our present and future financial health. We'll start with the basic mechanics.

---

6    Ibid.

# The Basic Mechanics of the Economy

While we tend to consider the economy to be extraordinarily complex, it actually operates in a very simple, predictable way. Transactions are the exchange of goods, services, or financial assets that occur between buyers and sellers. Individual markets are made up of everyone—people, businesses, banks, and governments—who is buying and selling the same type of goods, services, or assets. Those transactions and markets compose the economy.

There are three key players in this game. As Dalio eloquently explains in his book, "money serves two purposes: it is a medium of exchange and a store hold of wealth. And because it has two purposes, it serves two masters: 1) those who want to obtain it for 'life's necessities,' usually by working for it, and 2) those who have stored wealth tied to its value." The first group exchanges time for money, while the second "lends" their money in exchange for equity or assets like real estate, or with the premise that they'll eventually collect their initial investment and then some in the form of interest (more on this in a moment). The third player is the government, with the ability to participate in and exert control over the economy through policy making.

The government is the economy's biggest buyer and seller. It consists of two parts: a central government, which collects taxes and spends money, and a central bank, which controls how much money and credit are in the economy by affecting interest rates and printing new money.

Much of what we spend is actually credit, and it has big implications for your personal finances and the economy at large, making it worth your attention.

Credit is actually a form of money that is borrowed from tomorrow and spent today. To create credit, lenders and borrowers engage in the kinds of transactions mentioned above. To make more money on their money, they loan it to borrowers, who are usually trying to attain something out of reach. Thus, lenders provide borrowers with buying power in exchange for a promise to pay it back, with interest. In theory, this gives both parties what they're looking for: borrowers can make previously unaffordable purchases with the credit they receive from lenders, and lenders generate more money by earning interest on what they've loaned.

More spending is good for the economy. The money you and I spend is ultimately someone else's income. The baker, the butcher, the builder, the landscaper, the auto manufacturer, the auto dealer, the car salesperson—visualize how money multiplies in the economic system. But a point is reached when debt becomes too burdensome, and the borrower must pay it back. Along the path, the interest and principal expense becomes a greater portion of an individual's monthly budget. This leaves them with less to spend. Their personal economy slows. If this happens on a large scale, the overall economy slows. Less to spend is less money available to buy things.

But as soon as credit is issued, it immediately turns into debt—an asset to the lender and a liability to the borrower. The debt exists until that loan is paid back, at which point the transaction is considered settled and those assets and liabilities are no more.

Let's take a closer look at why credit is so crucial to the economy: In the United States, there is far more credit than money; there's about $1.5 trillion in currency in circulation, versus nearly $14 trillion in consumer debt.[7] Though they operate similarly, credit enables people to spend more than they make—for a while, that is. As we discussed in the first chapter, everything they spend becomes

7    "Key Figures Behind America's Consumer Debt," Debt.org, accessed February 26, 2020, https://www.debt.org/faqs/americans-in-debt/.

someone else's income, boosting those earnings higher: If you earn $100,000 and you don't have any debt, you'll be able to borrow an additional $10,000, and everything you spend—say it's the full $110,000—becomes someone else's income. With $110,000 in income, he or she is able to borrow a total of $11,000, and spend $121,000, and so on.

When an individual's income rises, he or she becomes more creditworthy. Why? Because he or she is better able to repay debts, thanks to the extra cash coming in and the assets he or she has. Thus, as income increases, so do borrowing and spending. Like a rock tossed into the pond, borrowing and spending ripple through the economy, creating growth. Credit can be good, enabling people to invest in goods and services that can allow them to repay that debt and grow their income. It can also be bad, causing people to spend more than they'll ever be able to repay. The real problem arrives when that debt can't be paid back.

To avoid that outcome and position both parties to benefit from the transaction, lenders and borrowers have to ensure that any newfound spending power is applied toward activities that will raise enough income to pay back debts. Sometimes, it's hard to strike a balance. Too-tight lending standards may lead to fewer debt problems but too little growth. Loose lending standards could lead to more growth but also create serious debt problems down the road, which would outweigh the benefits.

Unfortunately, our psychology gets in the way, and we act predictably poorly. Policy makers tend to be too loose rather than too tight with credit because they're focused on faster growth. In addition, being looser is easier than being restrictive, though it drives us to the place where many borrowers have taken on more debt than they can handle.

Without credit, our economy would only increase with productivity. As we learn and gain experience, we're able to be more productive, accomplishing more in less time. Our productivity increases slowly, but steadily. But since we have credit and the capability to borrow and spend more than we make with the promise to pay it back at a later date, we can boost economic activity above productivity now and decrease it in the future when it's time to repay that debt. This dynamic creates short- and long-term debt cycles.

It is income from work, retirement plans, social security, and investment savings, as well as borrowing (credit), that drives both short-term economic cycles and long-term cycles. And because borrowing on credit plays such a big role in societies, debt plays a critical role in the health of an economy and in those cycles. The short-term cycle occurs over the course of five to eight years, while the long-term cycle runs for seventy-five to one hundred years. As such, few of us have ever seen the end of a long-term debt cycle—the top of the last one was in the mid-1930s. And because we're typically focused on what's happening *now*—today, tomorrow, next week—we fail to notice the signs and symptoms of either cyclical pattern. But they matter.

Short-term cycles end in recession and reset. Long-term debt accumulation cycles are different. They are an accumulation of many short-term cycles, resulting in increased size and risk. You know you're near the end when debt relative to GDP (the measure of the market value of all goods and services produced) is more than 300 percent and the central bankers drop interest rates to zero. We'll take a closer look at these cycles and what they mean.

## The Short-Term Debt Cycle

To make things crystal clear, let's take the economic action down to the level of a single individual. We'll say he's your brother-in-law, and we'll name him John, just to personalize things a bit more. John is fresh out of school and lands a great job right out of the gate, earning $100,000. With a solid income and no debt, he can borrow an extra $10,000 in credit, allowing him to spend more than he earns. Multiply his case by hundreds of millions of people—all of whom can comfortably borrow and spend at the same moment in time. This kind of spending creates the first phase of the short-term debt cycle: expansion. There is more income than production, and we see inflation.

Individual desire and ability to borrow—your brother-in-law's included—depends on the attractiveness of interest rates. High interest rates dissuade people from borrowing, while low rates encourage them to do so. In the "How the Economic Machine Works" video, this is depicted as a government-controlled lever that can lower rates to stimulate borrowing and expansion and raise rates to cool things down and prevent inflation.

With the goal of keeping inflation in check, when borrowing heats up, the central bank increases interest rates. Those higher rates mean fewer people can borrow, since debt costs more. With less money and credit, they spend less. Incomes drop. Deflation happens next, and we find ourselves in a recession. The central bank doesn't want things to slow too much, so it drops interest rates again to get things moving.

Less interest means lower debt payments and increased spending and borrowing, and the short-term cycle starts all over again. But each time, there is more growth and more debt generated. That's because when they can, people choose to borrow and spend more, rather than working on their existing debt. And because we're focused on the here and now and everything appears to be humming along, they're able to. The factors people look at to judge the economy—incomes, asset values, etc.—are all rising. But we're creating a bubble, and it will eventually burst.

Let's check in on John to see what's happening at this point in the cycle. He's paid a little of that interest back. He's continuing to earn income. The banks like him. His credit score is improving. He's making a little more money. Now he can borrow more: $20,000, and the option seems appealing since interest rates are low. He puts that toward a new car. He's $30,000 in debt against his income. But he—and others like him—remains creditworthy because his income and asset values continue to rise, so lenders continue to lend. If John can refinance at lower and lower rates, he can stay in the game longer, and the cycle gets stretched. But because he's expanding his own economy through credit in addition to his income, at some point he'll top out.

## The Long-Term Debt Cycle

In the long term, debts outpace incomes. To manage their debt, people slow their spending. Less spending means others' incomes are lowered. With less income, their creditworthiness is reduced, limiting their capacity to borrow. Debts continue to grow, and spending plummets until we reach a point of no return where the debt burden is just too much to handle.

Debts continue to grow, and spending plummets until we reach a point of no return where the debt burden is just too much to handle.

During the short-term cycles, the Fed comes in and lowers interest rates, which lowers the cost of borrowing. But at some point, when the Fed Funds rate hits 0 percent, lowering interest rates no longer helps. People have just borrowed too much. By this point, John has $350,000 in debt, and his income has made little progress. He can't borrow any more, and he has so much in accumulated interest and principal to pay back. While he used to be able to spend all of his paycheck and then borrow and spend even more, a large portion of his income has to go directly to his debt. His personal economy begins to weaken, along with the economy at large.

Deleveraging comes next. Without the ability to borrow, he—and so many others—has to sell what he has, all while spending less. The presence of more available assets in the economy as people try to sell, along with less spending, causes the stock and real estate markets to plummet and banks to struggle. Since the value of their assets has gone down, people become even less creditworthy, and everything continues to tumble downward.

We need to do something, but we know that lowering interest rates has lost its effectiveness. Moreover, the debt burden is just too big. Lenders know they won't be able to recoup their money, so they stop lending. With the weight of the world on their shoulders, people stop borrowing too. They don't want any more debt. The only way to provide relief is to lower the debt burden, and there are four methods to make it happen:

- **Reduced spending on behalf of individuals, organizations, and governments.** This usually happens first. People cut down on their expenses to try to get a handle on their debts. The problem here is that when spending decreases, so do incomes. With lower incomes, people can't afford to pay their debts. Businesses spend less, too, cutting costs by eliminating extra personnel, leading to more unemployment.

- **Defaults and restructuring.** Lower incomes, higher rates of unemployment, and heavy debt burdens mean that many people have no way to pay back what they owe. As such, debts have to be cut. To avoid defaults and hang onto as many assets as they can, lenders allow for restructuring— either getting less money back, offering bigger time frames for repayment, or lowering previously agreed-upon interest rates. While this process reduces debt, income and asset values drop with it. The government struggles too, since less income means people owe fewer taxes. Simultaneously, more people are un- or underemployed and rely on the government for assistance. To provide necessary supports, the government has to spend more than it's bringing in via taxes, resulting in deficits. Strapped for cash, the government must find a way to generate more money, bringing us to the next step.

- **Redistribution of wealth.** The government seeks to fund its programs and support those who are struggling by raising taxes on the people who still have money. Tensions rise between those who are wealthy and those who are not. This can happen among classes within a single country, or between countries when one is reliant on the other for financial support, leading to political unrest.

- **The central bank prints new money.** Without the option to lower interest rates, the only thing left for the central bank to do is to print more money. To get that money into the economy, the central bank purchases assets. Purchasing assets helps to raise their prices, benefiting those who own them. The central bank can support those who don't own assets indirectly by buying government bonds. Doing so gives the government more spending power, which it puts toward stimulus programs and unemployment benefits. People's incomes increase, as does the total debt burden, though the government's debt continues to rise.

As you can see, some of these methods are inflationary and stimulate growth, such as printing money, while others are deflationary and help reduce debt burdens, like defaults and restructurings. From the point of no return, there are only two paths: the "beautiful" or the "ugly." Maintaining balance between each method of debt reduction allows for a much smoother process—the beautiful kind. When deleveraging is done well, incomes are growing faster on a percentage basis than the cost of the interest rate on borrowed money. For instance, if our income is growing at 4 percent per year and the base-lending rate is 2 percent, we can afford to pay off our debts. That gives people the potential to borrow again and spend more. But it's tricky to get it just right: incomes have to grow faster than debt, but growth can't be too quick. That requires printing more money, but not too much. And patience is key: when it's done right, it takes about a decade or so to reach equilibrium. What we don't yet know is what our elected officials and central bankers in the United States and around the globe will do. One thing that is clear is that we need to come together in a unified way. Will we?

At the end of his video, Dalio leaves the viewer with three rules of thumb to avoid personal debt crises as best they can: "First, don't have debt rise faster than income because your debt burdens will eventually crush you. Second, don't have income rise faster than productivity because you'll eventually become uncompetitive. And third, do all that you can to raise your productivity because in the long run, that's what matters most."[8]

Because of human nature, short- and long-term debt cycles in the economy are inevitable. Success depends on understanding how it all operates, where we currently sit in both cycles, and having the courage and conviction to place your bets. With that in mind, let's delve further into the short- and long-term cycles specifically and deepen our understanding of how to apply Dalio's template to evaluate our current condition.

---

8    Ray Dalio, "How the Economic Machine Works," Bridgewater Research Library, September 2013, https://www.bridgewater.com/research-library/how-the-economic-machine-works/.

# CHAPTER 3

# Short-Term Debt Cycles and Long-Term Debt Cycles

As we established in the previous chapter, there are short-term debt cycles—which you and I are most familiar with—as well as long-term debt cycles, which usually occur once in a lifetime. The latter is what we're most concerned with today. How did Dalio build a template to outline the probable outcomes of events few of us have ever seen? By carefully studying and plotting the course of history.

Believing that the past can tell us much about our future, Dalio and team studied forty-eight big debt cycles that led to depressions (which he defines as real GDP falling by more than 3 percent in large countries). Through this process, he "went through the erosion and eventual breakdown of the global monetary system ('Bretton Woods') in 1966–71, the inflation bubble of the 1970s and its bursting in 1978–82, the Latin American inflationary depression of the 1980s, the Japanese bubble of the late 1980s and its bursting in 1988–91, the global debt bubbles that led to the 'tech bubble' bursting in 2000, and the Great Deleveraging of 2008. And through studying history, [he] experienced the collapse of the Roman Empire in the fifth century, the United States debt restructuring in 1789, Germany's Weimar Republic in the 1920s, the global Great Depression and war that engulfed many countries in the 1930–45 period, and many other crises."[9]

With all this data in front of him, Dalio attempted to identify the cause and effect of events like business cycles and deleveragings, creating archetypal models of each. He also explored the unique characteristics of individual instances to understand what made one event different from the next. Through this process, he was able to gain "a simplified yet deep understanding of all these cases ... like an experienced doctor who sees each case of a certain disease unfolding as 'another one of those.'" [10] (Clearly, we've chosen the right practitioner!) From the research, he and his team built tools to inform Bridgewater's response to a slew of financial outcomes, including "a 'depression gauge' that was programmed to respond to the developments of 2007–2008, which had not occurred since 1929–1932."[11] His ability to recognize the pattern and respond accordingly enabled the firm to find success when most flailed.

His research also revealed that this short- and long-term debt cycle dynamic "has existed for as long as there has been credit, going back to before Roman times. Even the Old Testament described the need to wipe out debt once every fifty years, which was called the Year of Jubilee. Like most dramas, this one both arises and transpires

---

9    Ray Dalio, *Principles for Navigating Big Debt Crises* (Westport, CT: Bridgewater, 2018), 7.

10   Ibid.

11   Ibid.

in ways that have reoccurred throughout history."[12]

Centuries of research tell us that our position at any period of time has everything to do with debt and our ability to pay it back. As I write, I remain focused on the end of the long-term debt super cycle we are currently nearing. While it's new to most of us, it is not new to history. We've been here before.

Following is a chart of Total US Credit Market Debt from 1922 to December 31, 2019. Total Credit Market Debt is the total outstanding debt owed by all sectors (households, corporations, farms, state and local governments,

> I remain focused on the end of the long-term debt super cycle we are currently nearing. While it's new to most of us, it is not new to history. We've been here before.

the federal government, financial companies, and foreigners) and includes open-market paper, treasuries, agencies, munis, corporate and foreign bonds, bank loans, other loans and advances, mortgages, and consumer credit.

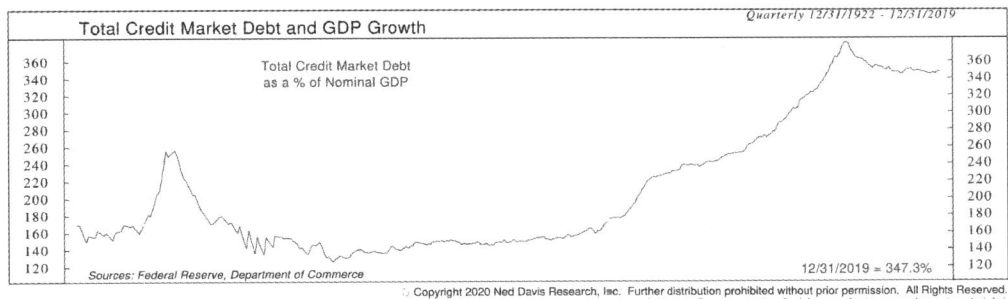

This looks ominous, but I'm not sharing it to make you scared.

---

12   Ibid., 14.

Knowledge is always your friend, and as investors, there are indicators we can follow to help us know when to de-risk. One of my favorite indicators is the NDR Credit Conditions Index. In short, it measures whether credit conditions are favorable (plenty of available liquidity to borrow) or unfavorable. Pay attention to the lower section of the chart and to the dotted line in particular. A drop below that line has preceded each of the last three recessions.

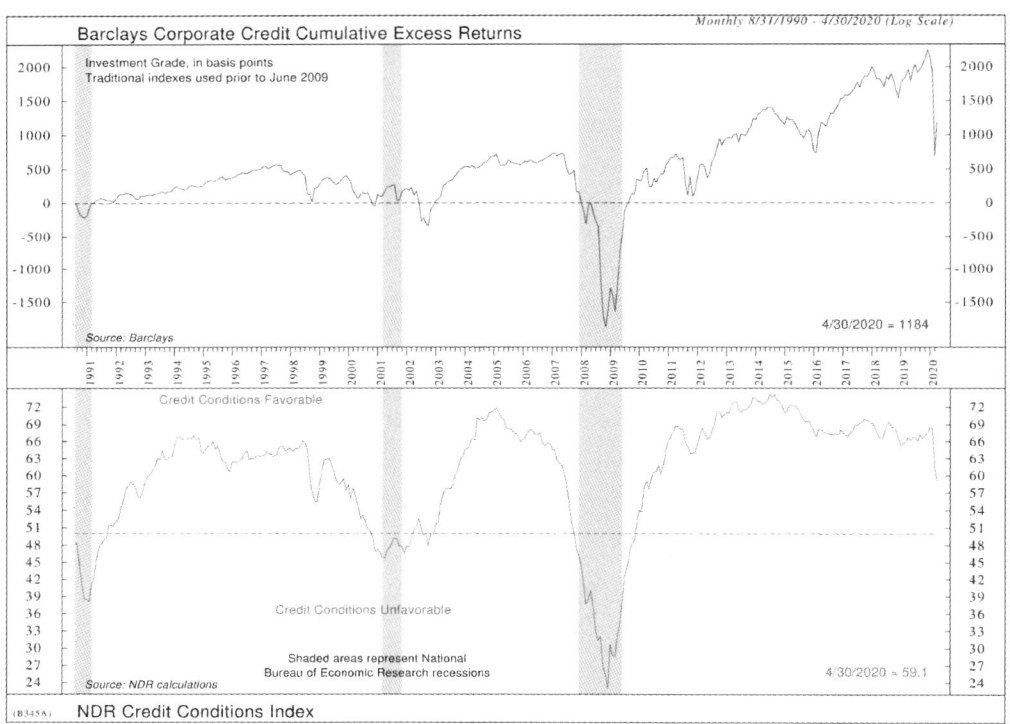

It's in recession that the bad stuff happens—debtors can no longer borrow, and defaults spike. As Dalio has shown, if we develop a better understanding of how past cycles have played out and where we are today, we can better navigate the period ahead. Each week, in a blog post I call *Trade Signals*, I post a number of my favorite recession-watch indicators. The NDR Credit Conditions Index is one of them. You can visit https://www.cmgwealth.com/ri-category/trade-signals/ to learn more.

Let's dig deeper into cause and effect: the short- and long-term cycles that create these patterns. Here, we'll build on what we learned in the previous chapter and see how Dalio's template can help us better pinpoint our position and do everything we can to create a beautiful deleveraging when the time comes. We'll start with short-term debt cycles.

## Short-Term Debt Cycles

Think back to your brother-in-law from the previous chapter. He started out earning a good income, gradually increasing his credit as he made payments and spent more. At first, his borrowing and spending were good for the economy, serving as someone else's income, and so on. During a short-term debt cycle, businesses and governments are all doing the same thing on the way up, fueling the economy as they go. We also learned that the way each player uses credit matters too: if they can increase their productivity thanks to what they borrowed, allowing them to pay back their debts and eventually raise their income, it's all good.

But human nature dictates that there are plenty of people and institutions that don't use credit productively and who will keep borrowing until they reach a point where they just can't do it anymore. Most of their earnings are going toward their debts. Their economies slow, and as they spend less, there's less for others to spend too. The worst debtors default, causing lenders to pull back and loan less. Recessions typically happen at this point. They're not great for the stock market—which drops about 37 percent on average—but they're a normal, healthy part of the economy.

At that point, the central bank can exert its power to pull economies out of recession by easing interest rates. Because people can borrow and spend again, the economy looks good again, and the cycle repeats. These short-term cycles occur over time—we've had at least one or two every decade since the 1950s. Each time we cycle, though, the highs are higher and the lows are lower.

## Long-Term Debt Cycles

Eventually we reach a point where too many people have gotten too much money too easily and the debt burden has become enormous. Incomes can't keep up with debt, and with interest rates at zero, central banks can't lower them to relieve the pressure. At that point, the short-term cycles add up to a long-term debt cycle.

In *A Template for Understanding Big Debt Crises*, Dalio shows what the end of a long-term cycle looks like with a chart depicting the United States' total debt burden since 1910. It highlights the fact that interest payments have held steady or declined even as debt increased, capturing the Federal Reserve's decisions to lower interest rates so that the economy can continue to grow on borrowed money—that is, until people can't afford to borrow anymore. He noted the years 1933 and 2008. They mark what Dalio believes to be the peak in the last two long-term debt cycles.

When the traditional strategy of lowering rates has lost its power, we find ourselves facing a severe debt crisis, and something new must be invented. Crises that ensue at the end of the long-term debt cycle fall into one of two categories: deflationary and inflationary. Deflationary depressions usually happen in countries that have financed their own debts. After interest rates hit zero, reduced spending and restructuring begin, but they're not countered with enough stimulatory efforts like money printing. Incomes continue to drop, restructuring isn't happening fast enough, and debt compounds as people take on more of it to make their payments. In the end, they have to sell their assets and default when they're no longer able to pay.

Inflationary depressions tend to happen in countries that depend on foreign capital flows and have a significant amount of debt expressed in other currencies. In these cases, less money and credit are coming in from other countries, and at the same time, inflation increases. Since much of the debt is denominated in a foreign currency, policy makers don't have as much control, creating a significant challenge. Which countries fall into this category? Turkey, Venezuela, and Iran serve as examples of countries experiencing inflationary depressions. Many Asian countries, including India, have large US-dollar-denominated debt as well. In addition, a number of European countries have debt that was converted from local currency to the Euro and are left with no ability to control their own currency.

While Dalio dissects both types of depressions in his book, we'll focus on deflationary ones, since much of the United States' debt is financed in its own currency. Luckily, that provides policy makers with more opportunity to mitigate some of the pain—if they play their cards right.

There are seven phases to this deflationary debt cycle: 1) the early part, 2) the bubble, 3) the top, 4) depression, 5) beautiful deleveraging, 6) pushing on a string, and 7) normalization. Let's go through the first few phases to get a better look at where we stand today—and what we stand to lose.

## 1) The Early Part

During the early part, debts are growing, but since those debts are helping to generate economic growth, incomes are still higher. Everything is relatively balanced. As such, this is often referred to as the "Goldilocks period."

## 2) The Bubble

A bubble begins to emerge as debts begin to outpace income, but those debts are still fueling asset returns and expansion. As Dalio explains, "this process is generally self-reinforcing because rising incomes, net worths, and asset values raise borrowers' capacities to borrow. This happens because lenders determine how much they can lend on the basis of the borrowers' 1) projected income/cash flows to service the debt, 2) net worth/collateral (which rises as asset prices rise), and 3) their own capacities to lend."[13]

Think back to your brother-in-law when he first set out, earning $100,000 and spending $110,000. His capacity to borrow was predicated in part on his credit, not just his earnings, which allowed him to continue to take on more debt for years. Long-term debt cycles can last for a very long time, since central banks continue to lower interest rates, "which raises asset prices and, in turn, people's wealth, because of the present value effect that lowering interest rates has on asset prices. This keeps debt service burdens from rising, and it lowers the monthly payment cost of items bought on credit."[14] At some point, as we know, those debt payments match or exceed the amount of money that people can earn and borrow; they simply can't pay them back.

The central banks are not exempt from the rampant optimism,

---

13   Ibid., 16.

14   Ibid., 17.

and as a result, they can add to the problem by failing to tighten the reins when they should. To develop a more effective perspective, Dalio believes that central banks need to focus on debt growth and its sustainability rather than focusing solely on inflation and growth. He explains that "central bankers sometimes say that it is too hard to spot bubbles and that it's not their role to assess and control them—that it is their job to control inflation and growth. **But what they control is money and credit, and when that money and credit goes into debts that can't be paid back, that has huge implications for growth and inflation down the road.** The greatest depressions occur when bubbles burst, and if the central banks that are producing the debts that are inflating them won't control them, then who will?"[15] To that I say amen.

## 3) The Top

How do you know when you're at the top of a bubble? It's pretty simple. As Dalio says, "When things are so good they can't get any better—yet everyone believes that they will get better—tops of markets are being made."[16]

Dalio lists seven factors as indicators for bubble formation based on his historical research, which are delineated in the chart below. He maps each factor to bubbles that occurred throughout history, further clarifying that individual circumstances in terms of ability to pay back debts across sectors must be taken into account.

I agree with the first five categories, and six is very much an affirmative: Household equity assets as a percentage of disposable personal income is currently at 155.99 percent. It was a record 153 percent in December 1999 and 133 percent in 2008. Margin debt

---

15   Ibid., 19.

16   Ibid., 21.

has reached a record high. Corporations have been aggressive buyers with repatriated cash and debt financing, some of which financed stock buybacks. Foreign buyers of US equities as a percentage of foreign-held US financial assets is higher than it was in 1999 and 2007. Only the 1950s and 1960s saw higher foreign ownership of US equities. As for number seven, "Does tightening risk popping the bubble?" The answer is *yes*!

Why is it so hard for investors to notice a market top? Perhaps it's a perverse sense of backward logic. Talking heads tell you how great the economy is doing and correlate that to higher asset prices. It feels safe, but under the surface, a bubble is nearing its peak. What may feel good is not really good at all. Recall the great Sir John's advice.

Usually, it's tightening by the central banks that causes the bubble to top out. As Dalio explains, "typical monetary policies are not adequate to manage bubbles, because bubbles are occurring in some parts of the economy and not others."[17] The banks can't keep up with the rest of the economy, and in areas that haven't yet been tightened, people are still borrowing, but they're doing so to pay back their debts—signaling unsustainability. When the bubble pops, asset prices are affected, causing lenders to worry they won't be repaid and to stop lending. Without credit, people have to sell what they have, reducing asset prices even further, and so on until the entire economy is headed for a reset.

Imagine all of this playing out in front of you as if it were a movie. Then imagine you've seen this movie before. You know the various plot points and potential outcomes. As such, you know the key characters to watch, understand the probable outcomes, and know who wins and who loses. Your investment success is dependent

---

17   Ibid., 20.

on how you defend your wealth and how you position it to grow.

As I write this book in late 2019, the question is: Are we near a top? Confidence is high, lenders are lax, individual households are fully invested in stocks, money-market asset levels are low, corporations have been borrowing and buying back their shares at record levels, investor optimism is high, valuations sit near record highs, the cyclical bull market run is the longest in history, and complacency is evident. We are also starting to see what Dalio refers to as "asset-liability mismatches" like investing in risky assets with borrowed money and borrowing and lending in different currencies.

Now pause the movie and grab some popcorn. Are things so good they can't get any better? Likely. This is the point where we find ourselves today, and it is eerily similar to the conditions seen at the last long-term debt cycle peak—with debt levels north of 300 percent and debt-to-GDP and interest rates near zero and even negative in much of the developed world.

Even though you're familiar with the plot, you may be swayed by what seems like a swell of positives. Everyone's cheering, and the herd mentality takes over—we humans tend to believe that, because everyone has bought in, we should too. Channel your inner Sir John Templeton and don't chase the herd.

If you are of the mindset that everything is rosy and there's nothing to see here, let me remind you that it always feels this good at the top. It's a debt-driven liquidity cocktail that is wonderful until it isn't. My message is simple: Seek growth, but do so with risk-management processes firmly in place. Better return opportunities will present, and a sound process will get you to them. Be patient.

## Paving the Way to Beautiful

With his template and the connections he makes throughout his book, Dalio is urgently trying to point out that we are dealing with a series of predictable events that happen at the end of long-term debt cycles. For a successful deleveraging, what Dalio calls beautiful, policy makers need to wake up and come together. That may not happen in a timely way. This is a point of significant consequence: there will be winners and losers.

Dalio believes that crises can be managed to avoid big problems, as long as they are denominated in the country's own currency, since in these cases policy makers have the ability to spread out the consequences, lessening their impact. If they can pull the right levers, they can save us all a lot of pain. Even in some of the worst cases, like the Great Depression of the 1930s, the impact was reduced once policy makers adjusted. Thus, it's not the debts themselves that create the biggest risks but policy makers' ability to manage them. To do this effectively, they have to have the knowledge and authority to use the tools at their disposal: reduced spending, restructuring, redistribution of wealth, and the printing of new money. They also need to understand how these changes will affect their various constituents and time the deployment of their tools accordingly since each one has different consequences and benefits for different parities.

Ultimately, I agree with Dalio's assessment. It's my belief that we are moving toward some form of global debt "jubilee." It will first require our legislators coming together and will then require global policy makers joining forces in a coordinated effort to forgive (write off) a portion of the debts. Printing, buying, and monetizing the debt. That will present a different set of challenges, so "beautiful" is really a relative word. We have put ourselves, as my dad used to say, "between a rock and a hard place."

Can policy makers come together? Perhaps, but I have my doubts that it will happen prior to a systemic shock. "Beautiful" remains a potential, but whatever path we take, it's going to get bumpy. You'll recall that Dalio, who bases every trade he makes on probabilities, said he puts the odds of a beautiful deleveraging happening at just 35 percent. In the meantime, he is urgently trying to educate global political leaders and central bankers on what's at stake and how to move forward. I'm praying for beautiful—and I remain hopeful. But know that ugly is quite possible, and could result in a 50–75 percent global market meltdown. For the optimist, that presents a good opportunity if you get the timing right.

As investors, we can get through it. By better understanding how the economy works, how debt cycles expand, and how they reach a critical point where they must contract, we can better anticipate and navigate the future. It's just a question of how we position ourselves and what we do. In this case, that means understanding why it's so important not to lose, or what I like to call "the merciless math of loss."

# CHAPTER 4

# The Merciless Math of Loss

One morning, my wife Susan and I were sitting in the kitchen, having our regular coffee, when she turned to me and asked, "If there was just one thing that I needed to know about investing, what would it be? What's the most important concept?"

It was a good question. Susan is no dummy—she's a Cornell grad after all—but the ins and outs of investments don't appeal to her. In essence, she just wants to know what matters most. And she's not alone. Many people take the same approach to investing that I do to my home's electrical system. They don't care about the intricacies of it all; they just want it to work.

"Well," I said, "you have to understand the power of compound interest. When you do, you'll realize that it's most important not to lose. Or to make sure that if you do end up losing, you only lose a little—not a lot."

"What do you mean?" she asked.

"The math doesn't work the same on the way up as it does on the way down. Here's an example. Let's say you have $100,000, and you lose 50 percent of your money. What kind of return do you need to get back to even?"

"50 percent," she answered.

"That's what most people think," I told her, sipping my coffee. "But let's walk it back slowly. You have $100,000. You lose 50 percent. What do you have?"

"$50,000."

"Okay, now you earn 50 percent on that $50,000. What do you have?"

"Oh my god," she said. "You have to teach everybody this!"

## The Merciless Math of Loss

What Susan learned that day is the idea behind what I call the *merciless math of loss*: when investments lose ground, they must make up much more of it percentage-wise just to catch up to where they started out.

The merciless math of loss explains Ned Davis Research's startling findings: that the average buy-and-hold stock market investor spends 74 percent of his or her time recovering from cyclical downturns in the market—three quarters of their time just getting back to the starting line!

> The average buy-and-hold stock market investor spends 74 percent of his or her time recovering from cyclical downturns in the market.

Say you invest $10,000 in the market, and your account takes a 10 percent loss over six months. You're down to a $9,000 balance. Because of your reduced capital base, you will have to earn 11 percent to recoup your losses. The steeper the losses, the higher the hurdle to break even becomes. For example, recovering from a loss of 30 percent requires a 42.9 percent gain. A 50 percent loss requires a 100 percent gain. To recover from a loss of 75 percent, a 300 percent gain is necessary! The following chart demonstrates the disproportionately high impact of losses.

### THE IMPACT OF LOSSES

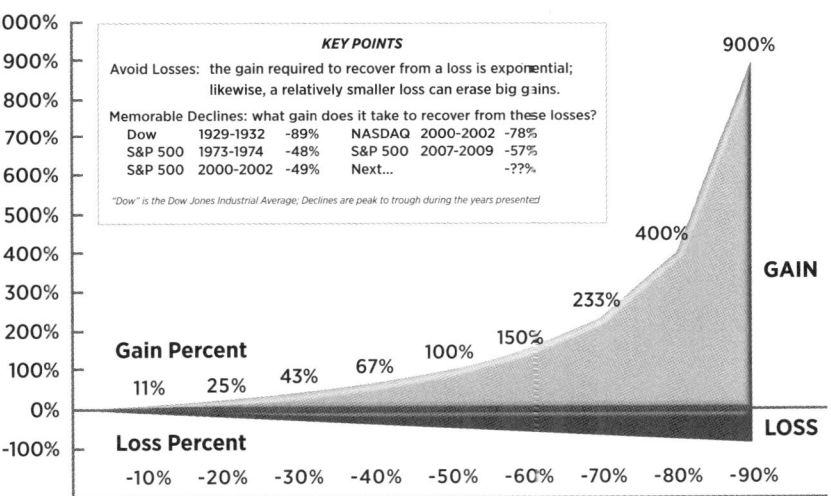

Getting back to even can also eat up precious time. Take that 10 percent loss over six months. Earning a steady 4 percent annually after that, you would still need another two and three-quarter years just to get back to where you started. That time would be much better spent accumulating new money. Remember, the idea is to grow your money, not just regain lost capital.

Spending time recouping avoidable losses makes investing extremely inefficient. For that reason, active investment management is critically important. This is where simple trend-following stop-loss risk-management strategies can help (more on that in Chapter 7).

Think of the various investment approaches as different types of aircrafts. Passive investments are like hot-air balloons. In favorable conditions, they can indeed carry passengers to their financial goals. But run into some bad weather and you're likely to find yourself stuck in a tree or plummeting toward the ground.

Active investments, on the other hand, are like planes. When winds are fair, they too can carry you in the right direction. They also have the flexibility to maneuver through bad weather, protecting their passengers from harm and keeping them moving toward their destination at a steady clip. Though many of us can see the benefits of choosing planes over balloons as a means of arriving at our final destination on time (and in one piece), it's not always easy for us to commit to this form of flight. Why?

It's not just the math that investors have to deal with; our psychology creates yet another hurdle.

## The Hurdle of Human Nature

As human beings, we're pretty evolved. We've certainly come a long way, with the ingenuity and agency to do incredible things. But unfortunately, we're still susceptible to thought patterns that have the potential to thwart our success—especially when it comes to money management. Over the years, a number of brilliant psychologists and economists have dug into our thought process surrounding money and the decision-making tendencies that can make us our own worst enemies in the world of investments. Let's take a brief look at what we're up against.

## The Psychology of Loss Aversion

*The aggravation that one experiences in losing a sum*
*of money appears to be greater than the pleasure*
*associated with gaining the same amount.*

### —Daniel Kahneman and Amos Tversky

We can turn to Israeli psychologists Amos Tversky and Daniel Kahneman to understand one of the primary instincts that leads us to less-than-optimal choices. Tversky and Kahneman studied the psychology behind judgment and decision-making, and Kahneman eventually won the Nobel Prize in Economics for their work. (Tversky would have likely shared the prize, but he had unfortunately passed away by then).[18] In the 1970s, they found that losses affect us twice as much as wins do, a phenomenon they deemed "loss aversion."

Kahneman would demonstrate the loss-aversion effect in the university classes he taught by simply flipping a coin. He would tell his students that if the coin landed tails up, they would lose $10. He then asked them how much they would have to win if it landed on heads to take the gamble. The answer? Twice as much as they risked losing: $20. He posed the same question to groups of executives—only this time they were at risk of losing a hypothetical $10,000. Time after time, the executives answered that they would have to have the chance to win at least $20,000 before the coin toss was worth their while.[19] As Kahneman and Tversky asserted, "The aggravation that one experiences in losing a sum of money appears to be

---

18  Ibid.

19  Erica Goode, "A Conversation with Daniel Kahneman; On Profit, Loss, and the Mysteries of the Mind," *New York Times*, November 5, 2002, https://www.nytimes.com/2002/11/05/health/a-conversation-with-daniel-kahneman-on-profit-loss-and-the-mysteries-of-the-mind.html.

greater than the pleasure associated with gaining the same amount."[20] In other words, the pain of losing $10,000 feels twice as strong as the joy of gaining $10,000.

What does this mean when it comes to human behavior? **Because we are more afraid to lose than we are excited about the possibility of gaining, we tend to behave irrationally.** We give more weight to situations where loss is a possibility, even when those situations are very unlikely. And we act accordingly, often to our own detriment.

> The pain of losing $10,000 feels twice as strong as the joy of gaining $10,000.

### The Advent of Behavioral Economics

Tversky and Kahneman's principle of loss aversion served as the backbone for the research of another Nobel Prize winner: economist and University of Chicago Booth School of Business Professor Richard Thaler. Thaler has been one of the pioneers of behavioral economics, the application of psychological principles to economic decision-making. He explores the irrational ways humans behave in economic situations and works to reconcile them with economists' faulty assumption that we are inherently rational.[21]

Over the course of his career, he has demonstrated that our economic decisions are affected by three factors: "cognitive limita-

---

20   Daniel Kahneman and Amos Tversky, "Prospect Theory: An Analysis of Decision Under Risk" *Econometrica* 47, no.2 (1979): p. 279.

21   The Committee for the Prize in Economic Sciences in Memory of Alfred Nobel, "Richard H. Thaler: Integrating Economics with Psychology," Royal Swedish Academy of Sciences, October 9, 2017, https://www.nobelprize.org/uploads/2018/06/advanced-economicsciences2017.pdf.

tions, self-control problems, and social preferences."[22] For example, the endowment effect, the concept that we ascribe more value to things we own than those we don't, falls under the category of cognitive limitations: we assign a higher value to something we already have than we would be willing to pay for it if we were to buy the same item from someone else.

Thaler conducted an experiment at Cornell University to illustrate the endowment effect. He passed out coffee mugs to students on campus. Some received the mugs and some didn't. Then he asked the students who had received them how much they'd charge for the mugs. Potential sellers valued the mugs at $4.75. Next he turned to those who hadn't received the mugs and asked them how much they'd be willing to pay for them. Their answer? Just $2.25. When we're selling something we've actually purchased, the concept of "anchoring" also comes into play: we tend to value an item based on what we bought it for, even if that item drops significantly in value (loss aversion dictates that you don't want to lose out, after all).[23]

Another issue we irrational humans tend to run into is the availability heuristic, our inclination to make a particular call based on the information that is most available to us, such as recent outcomes. Investors exhibit this behavior all the time. When we make a decision about whether to invest in something, we take in the whole history of the return. But once we put our money in it, we pay close attention to the day-to-day changes—every little move it makes. It's hard to watch those changes and not act based on the news of the day—even if we know that news doesn't matter.

---

22    Ibid.

23    Eshe Nelson, "The Flaws a Nobel Prize-Winning Economist Wants You to Know About Yourself," Quartz, October 9, 2017, https://qz.com/1098078/behavioral-economics-the-flaws-that-economics-nobel-prize-winner-richard-thaler-wants-you-to-know-about-yourself/.

Here, our myriad issues with self-control rear their ugly heads. Thaler's planner-doer model depicts our dual tendencies to behave based on instant gratification, all while worrying about that distant future. However, our desire for results *now* often leads us to overlook our long-term goals in favor of decisions that provide us with an immediate payoff—even when we know those choices will hurt us in the long run. (It's why—as Dalio's model shows—we're so willing to keep borrowing today, even when our future selves will almost certainly take a significant hit for the choice to carry more debt.)[24]

Thaler's status quo bias also factors into our decisions about whether to buy or sell. Because we are so afraid of loss, we are predisposed to stay the course, even if changing things up could mean big wins—or avoiding those losses in the first place.

## We're Our Own Worst Enemies

Strategist, value investor, and member of GMO's asset allocation team James Montier also explores the very human tendencies that often become fatal flaws for investors. In *The Little Book of Behavioral Investing: How Not to Be Your Own Worst Enemy*, he lays out the emotion, biases, and overconfidence that can create a perfect storm for investors' poor decision-making.

Montier explains that, while building a plan based on individual needs and interests and sticking to it is the best course of action, we often act on impulse—especially when we experience loss. In those situations, we typically do the opposite of what we should. Instead of buying during times when the market is basically on sale, we sell, following the crowd and hindering our potential for success.[25]

---

24   Ibid.

25   James Montier, *The Little Book of Behavioral Investing: How Not to Be Your Own Worst Enemy* (Hoboken: Wiley, 2010).

The inverse is also true: when things are looking good, investors become overly optimistic. They believe those wins will go on for eternity (which, of course, isn't true), contributing to the formation of bubbles. Confirmation bias plays a role here, too: people look for information that aligns with their existing belief system, ignoring anything to the contrary. When bubbles appear, they believe that this time things will be different, that returns will continue to skyrocket forever, rather than being wary of what seems like a continuous boom.[26]

As investors, these human traits can easily undermine our progress at every turn.

Finding success in investing is about minimizing the downside. That enables math to better compound on the upside. The key to long-term success is being able to make sure you can limit the really big mistakes. But to do that, we have to counter our own tendencies.

> The key to long-term success is being able to make sure you can limit the really big mistakes. But to do that, we have to counter our own tendencies.

## Navigating the Market's Inevitable Cycles

Why is it so important to heed the merciless math of loss and combat our own irrationality to minimize the downside? As we know from the previous two chapters, cycling is inevitable. Equities will grow over a long period of time at a relatively predictable rate. The problem is that over time, human behavior drives prices above and below that

---

26    Ibid.

long-term trend line. In a picture, it looks like this chart, courtesy of
Howard Marks:

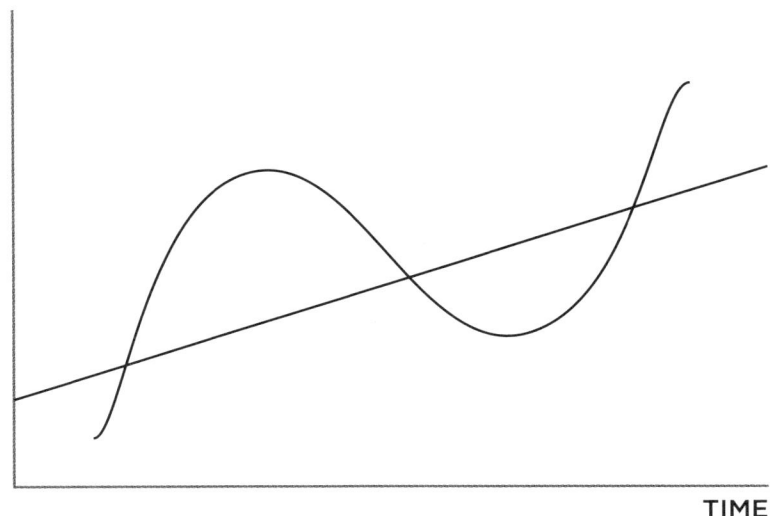

TIME

The rising diagonal line that moves from left to right represents
the equity return you receive over time. The line that peaks and
plummets above and below the equity return line is what happens
in real life.

We can look at this in real time. The dotted line in the middle
of this next chart is the long-term growth trend. You can see that
the price of the market moves above and below that trend over time.
What I like about this data is how it measures the distance from the
trend and plots it into five quintiles ranging from most overvalued
(above trend) to most undervalued (below trend).

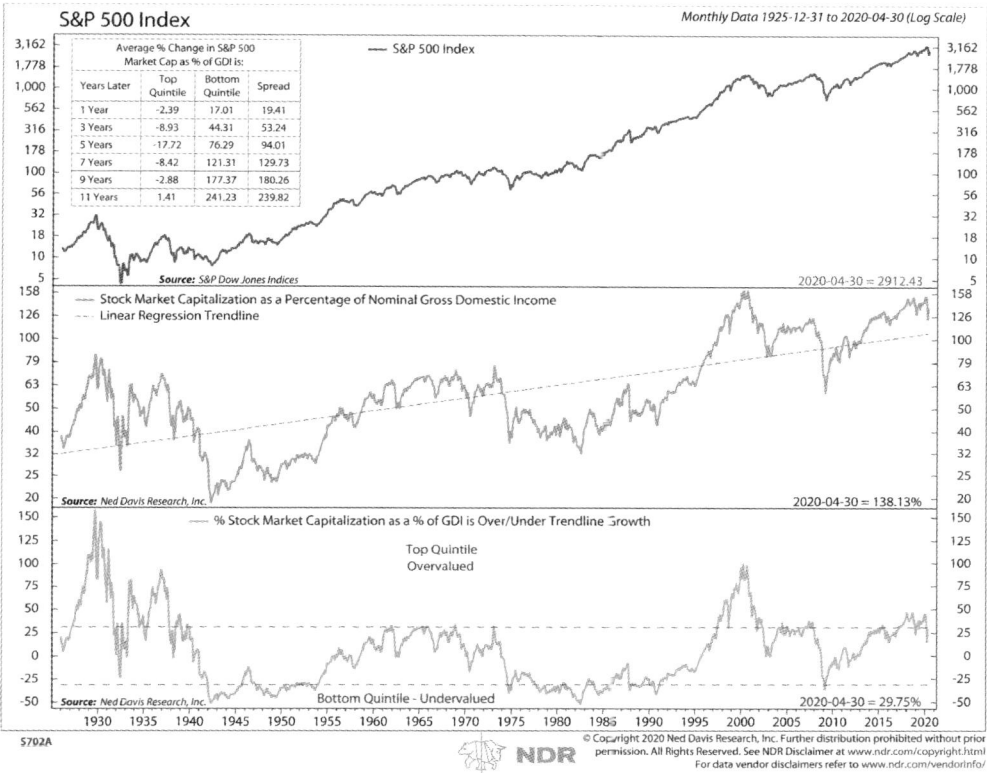

I think it is important to remember that all markets cycle over time. The top section of the next chart captures the monthly S&P 500 Average Price Index from 1900 through April of 2020. The second section shows government bonds, and the third section shows commodities. The shaded portions highlight bull markets and list the percentage return for the period of years highlighted. The nonshaded sections show bear market periods and the returns during those years. Looking at this chart, it becomes very evident that over time everything cycles, and you can see exactly why it's so important to manage your downside risk.

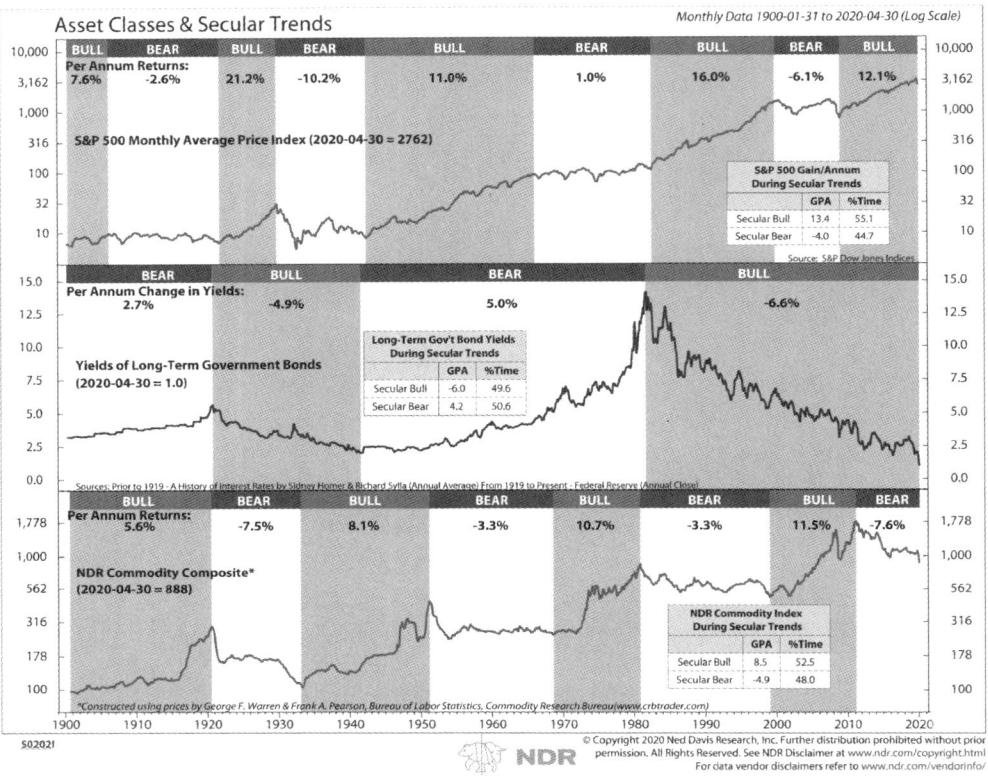

Asset Classes & Secular Trends

Monthly Data 1900-01-31 to 2020-04-30 (Log Scale)

As the chart demonstrates, the history of the markets is an ever-changing complex of opportunity and risk. Opportunity comes when panic selling drives prices below the long-term growth trend, and risk arrives when prices are bid up above the long-term growth trend. This is why an adaptive approach to investing is prudent. Knowing when to play more defense than offense or more offense than defense can aid you in defending and growing your wealth. But to truly understand how to navigate through these cycles successfully—when to play offense and when to play defense—you first have to understand recessions since they matter most. Let's talk about why.

# CHAPTER 5

# Recessions Matter

The greatest opportunities come during a crisis, and crises generally occur in recessions. Fear reaches an extreme, panic selling takes form, margin calls kick in, and buyers step away. The unwinding of leverage and investors fleeing equities drives prices lower. And that's when the best opportunities present themselves.

Years ago, when I was a young broker at Merrill Lynch, my manager tapped me on the shoulder and told me to get over to the Union League for a lunch presentation. "Yes, sir," I said, knowing little about the event. Two-hundred-plus brokers and advisors filled the historic downtown Philadelphia venue. Silverware was clinking against plates. The soft rumble of conversation resonated against the hall's leather, wood, and marble. But all heads picked up when the great Sir John Templeton took the stage. The famous Sir John was the founder of Templeton Funds and one of the great investors of the day. With pen in hand, I began to scribble notes.

Sir John began, "I'm going to give you the single greatest piece of advice I can give you. If you can master it, you will be one of the best brokers in the business. You should know, though, that while it sounds so easy, it will be one of the hardest things for you to do." The room grew still. I hung on his every word. He said, "The secret of my success is that I buy when everyone else is selling and I sell when everyone else is buying. And," he reiterated, "that will be one of the most difficult things for you to do."

It's been nearly thirty-five years since my lunch with Sir John. I believe it was the most important piece of advice I was ever given. Since then—whether it was the 1987 Crash, the 1991 Recession, the 1998 Long-Term Capital Crisis, or the Tech Bubble, the Great Recession/Great Financial Crisis of 2008–09, on the upside and the downside—investors have behaved badly. I'm often asked if the masses will change this behavior, and unfortunately my answer is always the same: no. But if you play your cards right, their panic and poor choices can work to your advantage the next time around—and the times that will follow.

Today we have an abundance of data we can use to help us measure "when everyone is buying" and "when everyone is selling." For instance, we can look at how much individual investors have invested in equities as a percentage of their liquid household net worth. There is also data on how much money mutual funds hold in cash. And we can conduct historical comparisons of how much money foreign investors have in US stocks. There are also investor sentiment surveys that help us gauge when investors have reached levels of extreme optimism (a bearish signal) and extreme pessimism (a bullish signal). But as significant as this information is in providing you with an edge, I believe what matters most is the timing of recessions. Think of a period "when everyone is buying" as an optimist's extreme, where the powder keg is fully loaded and ready to blow.

Think of recessions as the trigger that sets off the explosions.

Why do recessions matter so much? They reset the system. Weak companies default, the strong stewards of capital survive, pricing power is corrected, and a new expansion cycle begins. All but two of the major market corrections since 1916 have happened when there was a recession. And a number of them were quite painful: negative 40.1 percent, negative 46.6 percent, negative 47.9 percent and negative 86 percent. In the two recessions since January 2000, the market declined 50 percent each time. This is merciless math of loss in action: losing 50 percent and needing 100 percent to get back to even. Lose 75 percent, like many of us did in the Tech Bubble, and you're looking at 300 percent to get back to where you started. That's why it's so important to get out in front of recessions and be aware of the risks—and potential—they present. In the following pages, I'll show you how to avoid them.

When it comes to recessions, we run into yet another problem: The existence of a recession is defined by two consecutive losing quarters in a row. We only know we're in one roughly seven-and-a-half months after it has started. That's why, as we think about the impact of recessions, it's also important to understand the typical duration of bull and bear markets.

## The Length of Bull and Bear Markets

The chart at the end of Chapter 4 showed the long-term secular trend of the market—four long-term bear market periods

The existence of a recession is defined by two consecutive losing quarters in a row. We only know we're in one roughly seven-and-a-half months after it has started.

and five long-term bull market periods. Yet we investors live in the day-to-day. Putnam Investments has an excellent chart plotting the shorter-term mini cyclical bull and bear market cycles for the S&P 500 index that shows the magnitude and length of the cyclical bull and bear markets since 1949 (see opposite page). Secular simply refers to long-term cycles and cyclical means short-term cycles.

There are several observations from Putnam's data. Bull markets almost always last longer than bear markets and almost always gain more in percentage terms than bear markets lose. Eight of the fourteen cyclical bull markets gained between 60 percent and 100 percent, three gained between 39 percent and 59 percent, and three were spectacular: +407 percent (1949–1956); +281 percent (1982–1987); and +526 percent (1990–2000).

Meanwhile, the smallest bear market decline was -8 percent in 1960. Five bear market declines ranged from -14 percent to -17 percent; three ranged from -22 percent to -29 percent (the most recent bear markets have been two of the worst, with losses of 43 percent and 51 percent in 2000–03 and 2008–09, respectively).[27]

The duration of bear markets is shorter. Five of the bear markets lasted less than ten months, seven lasted between fourteen and twenty months, and one lasted thirty months. The median length for recessions is ten months, with the shortest clocking in at six months and the longest lasting eighteen months. It's a matter of months, not years. Because the window is small and markets peak prior to recessions and decline as they occur—and because they bottom prior to and rally during expansions—it's important to have a process in place that enables you to take action.

---

27  "Bull Markets Dominate Bear Markets in Length and Returns" *Validea's Guru Investor Blog*, September 7, 2015, http://blog.validea.com/ bull-markets-dominate-bear-markets-in-length-returns/.

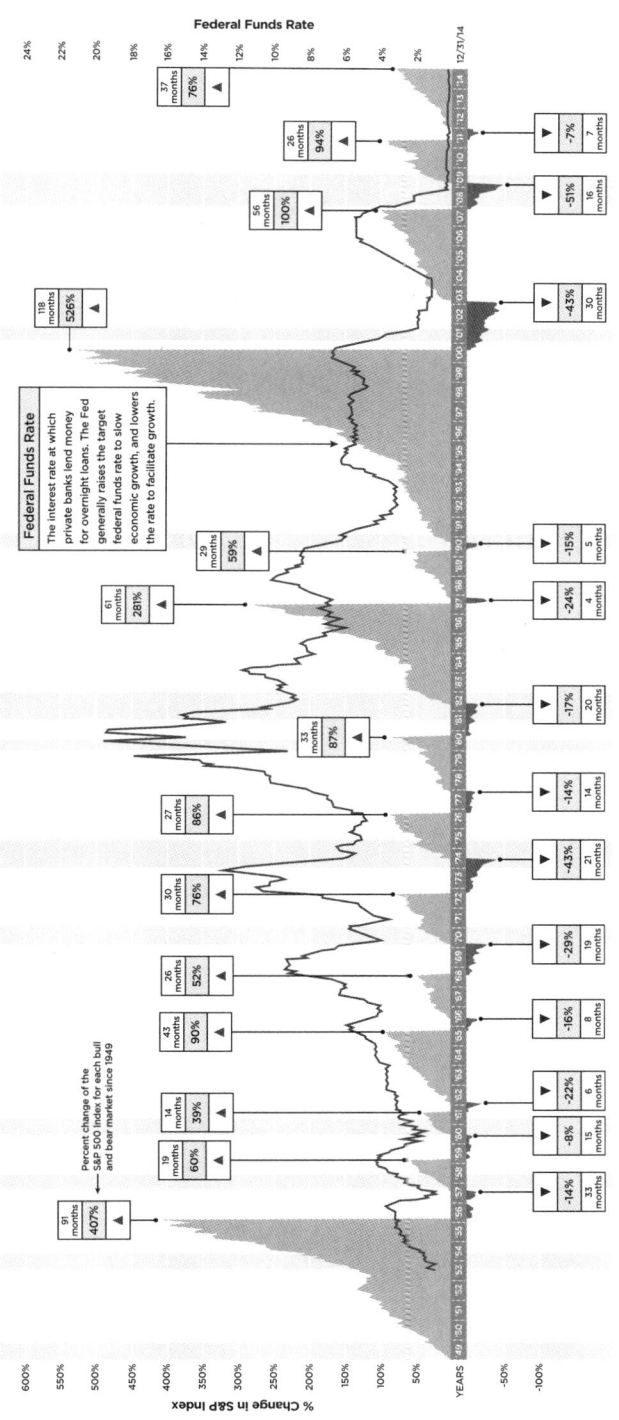

Federal Funds Rate

Federal Funds Rate

The interest rate at which private banks lend money for overnight loans. The Fed generally raises the target federal funds rate to slow economic growth, and lowers the rate to facilitate growth.

Percent change of the S&P 500 Index for each bull and bear market since 1949

% Change in S&P Index

YEARS

When change is on the horizon, the stock market and the economy set off a series of signals. If we're tuned in, we can better adapt to minimize losses—and position ourselves to gain from the attractive return opportunities that recessions create. Luckily, there are a number of factors that you can use to identify recessions and expansions.

# Recession Signals: The Indicators to Watch

So how do you know when a recession is nearing? The first—and most basic—factor is timing. As of December 2019, the current economic expansion, which began in 2009, turned 127 months old, making it the longest in history, eclipsing the 120-month expansion (1991–2001) that ended with the Great Tech Crash. Looking back more than one hundred years, you'll find that the average expansion has been forty months. All expansion cycles end with a recession. The current record 127-month economic expansion cycle is aged. Odds favor a recession in 2020, but that's certainly not guaranteed.

I created a dashboard of indicators to help me monitor the economy each week. On my *Trade Signals* blog, I post a series of my favorite recession-watch indicators. I believe they can help you and me both better identify turning points. Let's take a look at some of them:

## The Economy Based on the Stock Market Indicator

Seasoned investors know that the stock market is one of the best leading indicators of what's to come. People tend to believe that the stock market is reflective of the economy, that it looks good when the economy is doing well and vice versa. But that's not actually how it works. Investors are always looking forward. We're trying to determine the potential for companies to drive growth. Sometimes, at the peak of a cycle—especially prerecession—companies' earnings start to roll over, sending out a series of signals. Millions of us investing with our dollars start to pick up on these signals and proceed accordingly.

One indicator that's been right 75 percent of the time since 1948 is the Economy Based on the Stock Market Indicator. An expansion signal is generated when the S&P 500 rises above its five-month smoothed moving average by 3.6 percent. A contraction (recession) signal is generated when the S&P 500 declines below that smoothing average by 4.8 percent. Economic activity accelerates above trend when the stock market is strengthening, and conversely it slows below trend—or contracts—when the stock market is underperforming. What's interesting about this process is that it has correctly forewarned of every recession since 1970. It's also done an excellent job in identifying expansion periods. You can find the data updated monthly in my *Trade Signals* blog.

## Recession Probability Based on Employment Trends

The Conference Board Employment Trends Index data is published monthly, and it's worth your attention. It takes into account eight different indicators—including claims for unemployment insurance, the percentage of firms with positions they have been unable to fill, job openings, and real manufacturing and trade sales—for an accurate read on the current employment environment in the United States.[28] This, too, is valuable data, and it's sending its own message about recession risk. When the Employment Trends Index begins to rise by 0.4 percent from a low point, it generates an expansion signal. Some recession signals have triggered shortly after a recession began. Nevertheless, data from 1979 to May 2020 shows that this

---

28 "The Conference Board Employment Trends Index," The Conference Board, accessed March 11, 2019, https://www.conference-board.org/data/eti.cfm.

process has had a 100 percent track record of calling every economic recession and every expansion. The process signaled recession in early 2008 and an expansion in late 2009. The latest signal, at the time of this writing, is a recession signal triggered on April 30, 2020.

## Credit Conditions Index

Credit conditions are also an excellent indicator of recessions. This one is pretty simple. If you want to borrow, whether it's to acquire more credit or to secure a loan to buy a house, is the money easy to get? You'll remember that the economic system is fueled by the spending of income and credit. When lending conditions are favorable, the economy does well. When lending conditions are unfavorable—and liquidity dries up—the economy runs into trouble. Ned Davis Research Credit Conditions Index plots the data back to 1990. Readings above fifty mark Favorable Credit Conditions, and readings below fifty signal Unfavorable Credit Conditions. There have been three recessions since 1990. While that does not make for a large data set, credit conditions became unfavorable just prior to each of those recessions. It's when lending dries up that overleveraged businesses and individuals find it hard to gain further funding or rollover existing debt. That's why this indicator is so important.

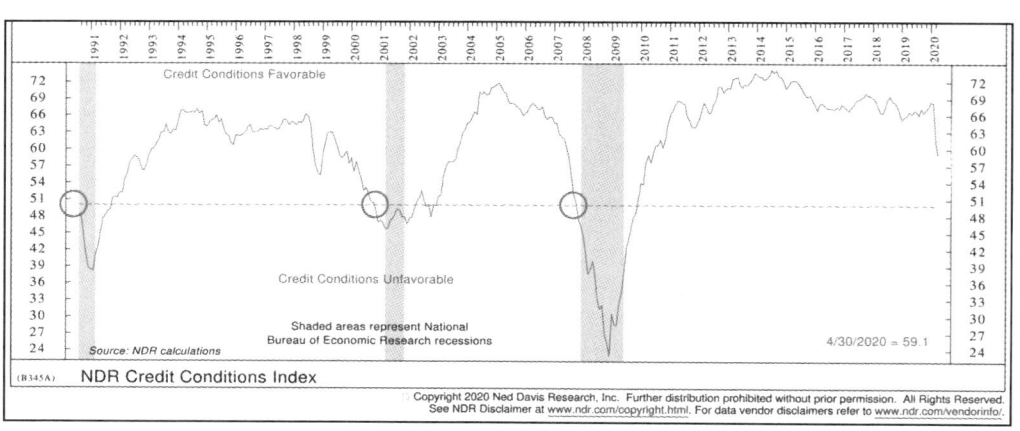

## US Economy vs. Yield Curve

The US economy versus the yield curve is by far the most popular recession-watch warning indicator in the business. It compares the difference in the six-month Treasury bill yield to the ten-year Treasury note yield. When the short-term yield moves above the longer-term yield, it's known as an inverted yield curve. This is an unusual occurrence, one that tells us something is wrong in the economy. It signals that the economic patient has the flu or perhaps something more serious.

This indicator has predicted every recession since 1958. It's an early warning sign, generally occurring months before the fireworks go off. Recession usually follows between seven and twenty-one months later, with the median lead time being fourteen months. You typically have about a year's warning time from inversion to the time of recession.

Recession began twenty-one months after the yield curve inverted in 2006. The stock market peaked in October 2007. Few saw it coming. The stock market went on to lose more than 50 percent during the Great Financial Crisis (2007–09).

The most recent yield curve inversion occurred in April 2019. It indicates that a recession will occur by the summer of 2020. As of May 2020, that warning appears prescient. Keep an eye on this excellent watch signal, and when it drops below zero, get your ducks in order. Just one of the ten occurrences since 1958 did not result in recession. Nine did. The odds are difficult to ignore.

Just like the flu, recessions are contagious. If the whole world has a fever, chills, nausea—the works—many others are likely to come down with it next. This is why it is also important to gauge the global economy. The NDR Global Recession Model is a global composite of leading indicators (CLIs), created by OECD, covering thirty-five countries. Each CLI contains a wide range of economic indicators such as money supply, yield curve, building permits, consumer and business sentiment, share prices, and manufacturing production. There are usually five to ten indicators, which vary by type and weight, depending on the country, and are selected based on economic significance, cyclical behavior, and quality.

The NDR Global Recession Probability Model incorporates both the CLI level and trend data of all thirty-five countries to predict the likelihood of a global recession. A score above seventy indicates that the risk of recession is high, while a score below thirty means the risk is low. The NDR Global Recession Probability Model is a forward-looking model using a two-month lead in the CLI data. Since periods of recession can only be known in hindsight, warning indicators such as NDR's Global Recession Probability model can help us assess the global growth conditions and signal when to become more defensively focused.

In July of 2018, the risk of global recession was approximately 59 percent. In December 2019, the risk of recession reached a probability of 96 percent. In May 2020, there is a high probability that the balance of the globe, including the US economy, is in recession. Two consecutive quarters of negative GDP growth are required to confirm recession. The recession indicators are helpful, though, and fortunately we have models like this that can help us get in front of recessions before those chills come on.

You can find the recession charts, updated monthly, at https://www.cmgwealth.com/ri-category/tradesignals/. Equipped with the recession indicators to watch out for, it's time to talk about how to put a game plan in place: an adaptive investment mindset that balances offense versus defense, tackling what Sir John Templeton described as one of the hardest tasks in this business. But with the right tools—and the knowledge and discipline to overcome our natural-born tendencies to behave badly—you're primed to win. How do you create your game plan? Read on.

# CHAPTER 6

# Balancing Offense vs. Defense

Y ou no doubt know the name of investing legend Warren Buffett. It's not just his career that's legendary; it's also his eating habits. Buffett's penchant for Coca-Cola, See's Candies, and salt—and his corresponding disinterest in vegetables— are well documented. As he explained, "I checked the actuarial tables, and the lowest death rate is among six-year-olds. So I decided to eat like a six year old. It's the safest course I can take."[29] Given his track record, you may find yourself reaching for a Coke (or five).

One of his favorite foods—unsurprisingly—is hamburger meat. As we begin our discussion of when to play more offense and when to play more defense, we can look to Buffett and his appreciation of the kid-friendly food. In an interview with *Fortune* magazine, he shared a little inside baseball regarding both his investment strategy and his love of hamburgers. "To refer to a personal taste of mine,"

---

29   Patricia Sellers, "Warren Buffett's Secret to Staying Young: 'I Eat Like a Six-Year-Old,'" *Fortune*, February 25, 2015, http://fortune.com/2015/02/25/warren-buffett-diet-coke/.

he said, "I'm going to buy hamburgers for the rest of my life. When hamburgers go down in price, we sing the 'Hallelujah Chorus' in the Buffett household. When hamburgers go up in price, we weep. For most people, it's the same with everything in life they will be buying—except stocks. When stocks go down and you can get more for your money, people don't like them anymore."[30]

If it's as straightforward a process as purchasing hamburger meat, why do investors shy away when prices get low? As we established in Chapter 4, fear replaces reason, time after time. We saw it happen in 2001–02 and again in 2008–09 and many times prior. But if you can overcome that fear—and like Buffett, sing when prices go down—you can take advantage of it. The price you pay for an asset matters! There is a disciplined way to make valuations and stock ownership work in your favor.

Buffett's simple insight is right in line with the life-changing advice I got from Sir John Templeton at that fortunate lunch meeting in 1985: that it's most prudent to buy when everyone else is selling and sell when everyone else is buying. But as Sir John warned, it's just not as easy as it sounds. That's why I believe you have to create a process that removes emotion.

The goal of every investment portfolio is to capture growth while preserving capital—simple enough, right? Yet, these two goals are at odds with each other. Taking on too much risk to increase returns, or growth, risks large losses. Being too conservative to prevent loss, or preserve capital, stymies growth. The trick is to find the right balance. You have to know when to play more offense than defense and when to play more defense than offense.

That's where understanding equity market valuations and what

---

30   Carol J. Loomis, "The Wit and Wisdom of Warren Buffett," *Fortune*, November 19, 2012, http://fortune.com/2012/11/19/the-wit-and-wisdom-of-warren-buffett/.

they tell us about coming returns comes in. Valuations can tell us very little about timing the peaks and troughs in the bull and bear market cycles, but they can tell us a lot about the returns we are likely to receive years down the line. In short, like the price of hamburgers—your current investment starting conditions matter.

**Taking on too much risk to increase returns, or growth, risks large losses. Being too conservative to prevent loss, or preserve capital, stymies growth. The trick is to find the right balance.**

## Starting Conditions Matter

Your starting conditions can and should serve as a guide to help you position your portfolio for the period ahead. Starting investment conditions can tell us a great deal about coming three-, five-, seven-, ten-, and twelve-year returns, as well as risk levels.

To set the stage, consider those bull and bear market cycles. We love bull markets and loathe bear markets. Both happen. And they differ in length and magnitude—recall the earlier chart detailing the bull and bear market secular trends since 1900.

During the approximately 55 percent of the time that we are in bull markets, returns are up and investors are happy. During bear markets, investors are not. And unfortunately, those long-term secular bear market cycles can last a number of years, a reality that's very difficult for many investors to stomach. For instance, if you invested $100,000 in the S&P 500 in 1966, you would have averaged approximately 1 percent returns for the next sixteen years or so. That's not good. The starting conditions in 1966, 2000, and 2007 were poor. The opposite was true in 1982, 2002, and 2009.

Next is a look at the Dow Jones Industrial Average over the same long-term time period. From 1966 to 1982, the Dow Jones Industrial Average lost 1.5 percent per year before factoring in inflation. After inflation, the return was -7.9 percent per year. You may remember the greatest Fed chairman in history, Paul Volker, and his successful fight against inflation. That was a different investment environment, one that many investors today never experienced. Sixteen years averaging negative 1.5 percent per year is a long and painful run. Compounding investor pain was the inflation pressures of the 1970s and early 1980s.

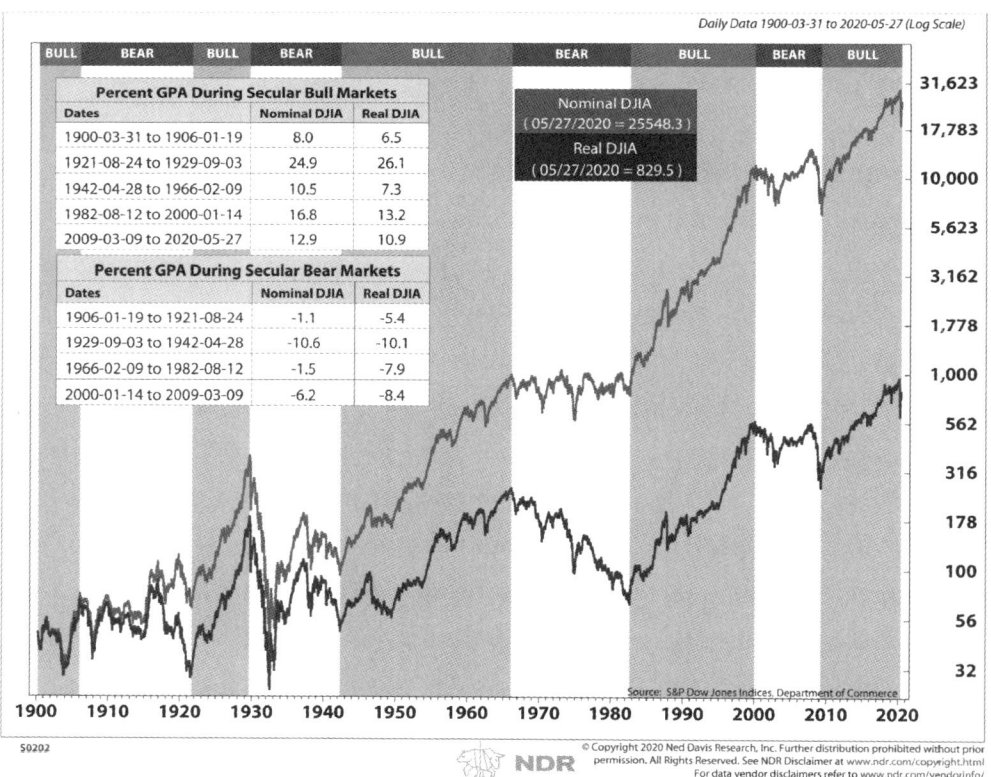

GMO's Jeremy Grantham, famous for calling the last two bubbles, was on CNBC in March 2019 saying, "Don't expect a massive drop to signal the end of the longest bull market in history. This will be limping along; three steps down, two steps back. It's not a typical experience. I was really hoping there would be a magnificent bubble ending to this, as there had been to the three great recent experiences. It doesn't look like it will and, therefore, you're going to have a decline of a different nature."

He may be right. With valuations high and the bull market aged, the point I'm hitting hard is that risk is high and coming returns will be low. This year, next year? Don't know. What about over the coming five to twelve years? I think you'll find the valuation and return data that follows to be compelling.

## The Game Plan

Play more defense than offense when valuations are richly priced and equity markets sit late cycle—above its long-term growth trend. Play more offense than defense when prices are low and sit below their long-term growth trend. Put processes in place that enable you to systematically grow and defend your wealth—that's what matters. But how do you make sure you're getting the opportunity to play offense with your money intact?

If you are in your twenties or thirties, simply find a good ETF that gives you the market at a low cost, keep adding money every year and dollar-cost average for the next thirty years. When the next recession resets valuations, don't worry—stick to the long-term game plan and add more.

However, if you are a preretiree or retiree like me, we just don't have the same time runway. It can take a while to recover from a bear market, especially when inflation is factored in. We can't afford to wait the years necessary to overcome another 50 percent loss on our retirement savings. For example, imagine you are fifty, sixty, or seventy years old and it is December 1999. You're planning to retire in the next ten to fifteen years. Initial starting conditions matter, whether preretirees know it or not.

Here's how it played out for the preretiree or retiree who turned sixty years old in 1999. The top line shows the Dow Jones Industrial Average, the middle line shows the S&P 500 Index, and the bottom line shows the NASDAQ. Note the long period of time spent below 0 percent, or underwater (nearly twelve years for the Dow, thirteen years for the S&P 500, and sixteen years for the NASDAQ).

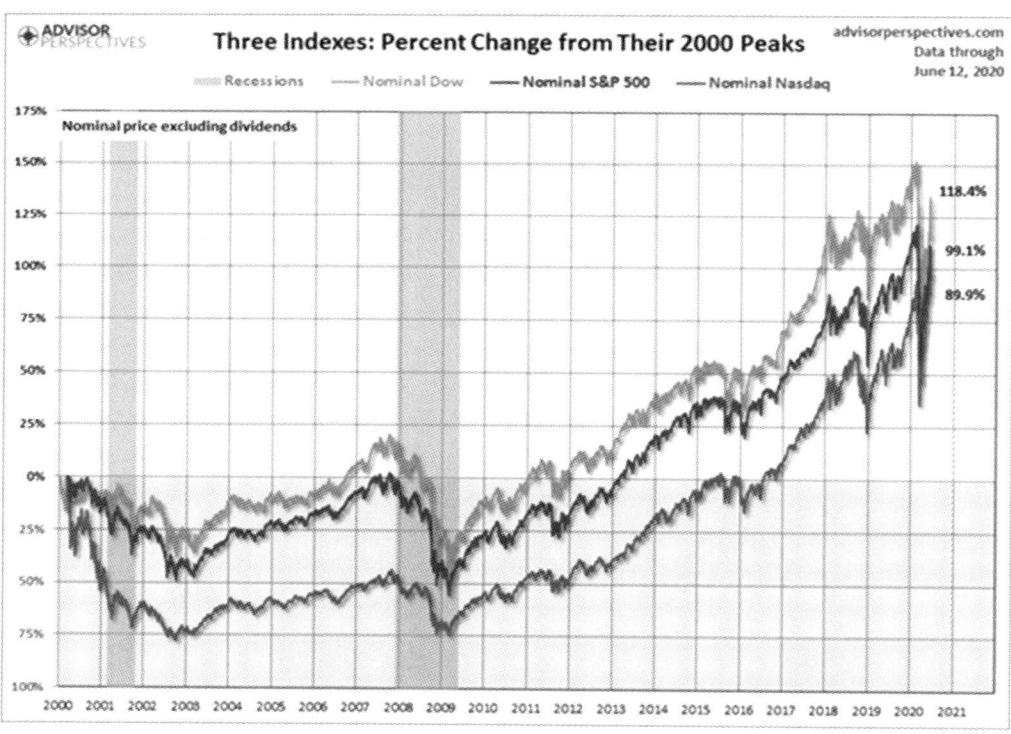

And it is important to factor inflation into the equation. Inflation matters, since we need our money to grow in order to buy things that inflate in price over time.

Here's the same chart after inflation is factored in.

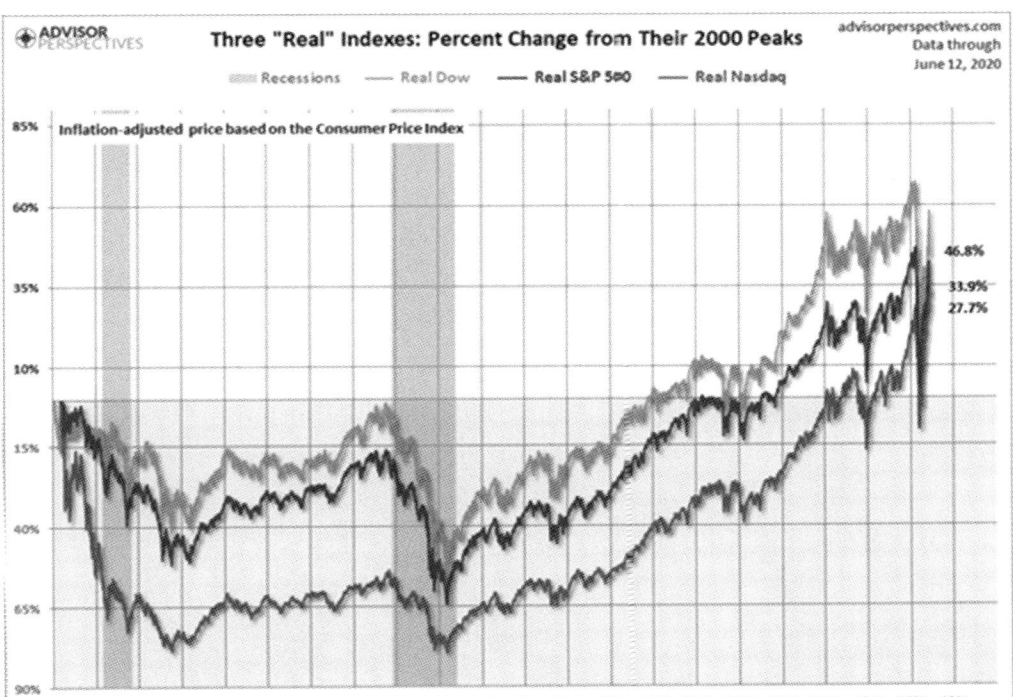

I'd argue that those of us approaching or in retirement are facing a similar situation today. The stock market is richly priced, suggesting it's time to play more defense than offense. Fourteen years, after inflation is factored in, is a long time to go without earning a return. Age sixty to age seventy-four with no net gains changes the retirement picture. Given the current late-cycle low return environment, until valuations reset lower, I suggest a more adaptive investment approach.

Now, note the vertical gray bars in the previous chart. They capture the last two recessions. As we discussed, recessions tend to clean house. Stock markets decline significantly and subsequently create new investment opportunities. They drive down the price of hamburgers. Before we cover ideas on how you can create a defensive plan to protect your wealth, let's look at some important indicators that can help you identify when, like the members of the Buffett household, you should get excited and sing.

## Valuations and Coming Returns

Valuations can help us determine what to do and when to do it. So it's time to put your geek cap on. We'll take a closer look at some different valuation metrics and compelling coming return data. Keep Buffett's quote on hamburgers in mind, as the data here backs that up.

### S&P 500 Index Median P/E

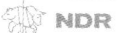

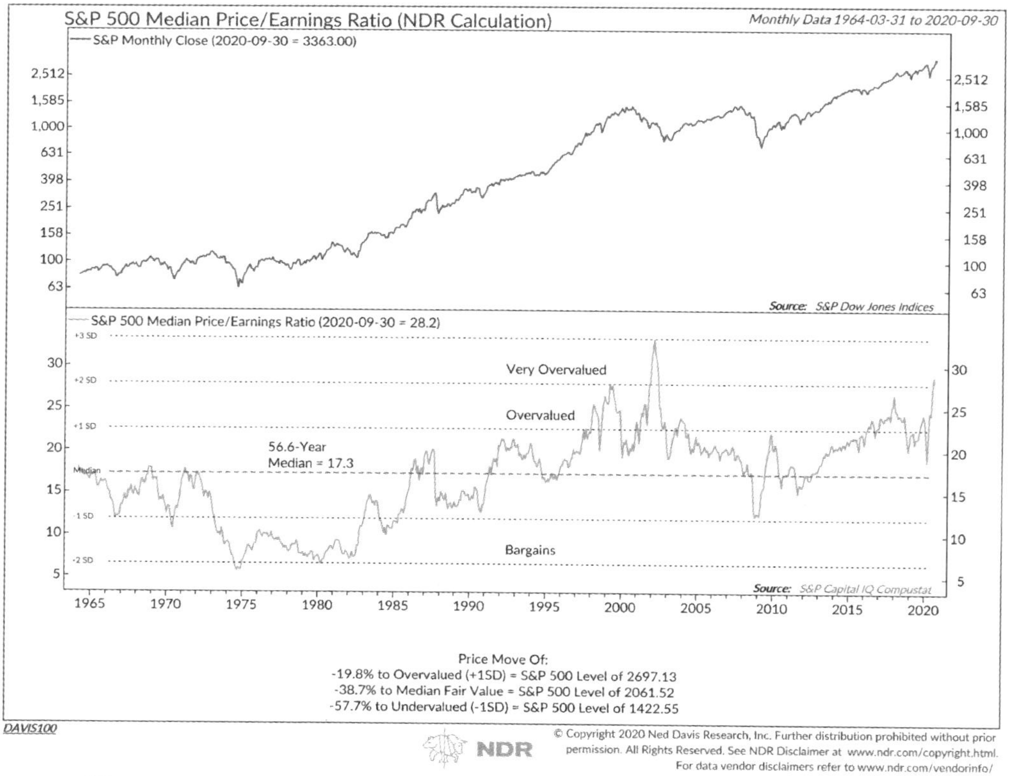
S&P 500 Median Price/Earnings Ratio (NDR Calculation)
Monthly Data 1964-03-31 to 2020-09-30
S&P Monthly Close (2020-09-30 = 3363.00)
2,512
1,585
1,000
631
398
251
158
100
63
Source: S&P Dow Jones Indices
S&P 500 Median Price/Earnings Ratio (2020-09-30 = 28.2)
+3 SD
+2 SD
+1 SD
Median
-1 SD
-2 SD
Very Overvalued
Overvalued
56.6-Year
Median = 17.3
Bargains
30
25
20
15
10
5
Source: S&P Capital IQ Compustat
1965
1970
1975
1980
1985
1990
1995
2000
2005
2010
2015
2020
Price Move Of:
-19.8% to Overvalued (+1SD) = S&P 500 Level of 2697.13
-38.7% to Median Fair Value = S&P 500 Level of 2061.52
-57.7% to Undervalued (-1SD) = S&P 500 Level of 1422.55
DAVIS100
NDR
© Copyright 2020 Ned Davis Research, Inc. Further distribution prohibited without prior permission. All Rights Reserved. See NDR Disclaimer at www.ndr.com/copyright.html.
For data vendor disclaimers refer to www.ndr.com/vendorinfo/

Let's start with a look at the S&P 500 Index Median P/E Chart. Median P/E chart—my favorite valuation chart. Of the 500 stocks that make up the S&P 500 Index, median refers to the P/E in the middle. Half the stocks have a higher P/E and half a lower P/E. I'm particularly fond of this method because it tends to eliminate one-time accounting gimmicks. It also allows us to look at where we have been historically and determine now the market did ten years later. Thus, we're putting real-life performance stats to Buffett's hamburger theory.

The dotted line in the bottom half of the chart marks the 56.3-year average Median P/E. Think of that number as the "fair value" for the price of the market relative to its earnings over time. When the Median P/E drops to this line, hamburgers are fairly priced. There are periods of time when the market is undervalued—such as 1982, 1992, and 2009—and when it is overvalued—like 1966, 1987, 1999, and 2007. Note the Median P/E ratio at the end of April 2020 is lower than it was in mid-2018 but remains higher than it was in 2007, the late 1990s, and the early to mid-2000s.

The bottom section of the chart helps us set some targets. For example, should the S&P 500 decline 38.7 percent from 3,363.00—the level it was at on September 30, 2020—to 2,061.52 (Median Fair Value), that would be a good time for investors to sing. Investors might even consider throwing a big party if a 57.7 percent correction takes the S&P to the "undervalued" level of 1,422.55. That would be an outstanding level to meaningfully overweight stocks, even if you are a retiree. Absent another recession, a 19.8 percent decline to 2,697.13 is probable in my view. With recession, it is possible the market could decline to the "undervalued" level, that 1,479.53. The bottom line here is **when you're looking at Median P/E, set your sights on the dotted "fair value" line. When this metric**

**is showing that the market is overvalued, simply tighten your stop-loss triggers. Play more defense than offense until valuation improves.** One last note on Median P/E. Over time, the S&P 500 Index has provided an annualized return of approximately 10 percent per year. I like to think of Median Fair Value as the point at which I can expect that 10 percent. Fairly priced hamburger meat. Please note that playing defense doesn't mean abandoning your offensive strategy altogether. We'll soon look at a few simple trend-following strategies that enable you to continue to seek growth *while* you minimize your risk of loss.

Understanding price relative to earnings can help you clearly see where we sit in the cycle and what that tells you about coming returns and levels of risk.

## What Median P/E Tells Us about Forward Ten-Year Returns

Recall that we considered Median P/E in thinking about my wife Susan's soccer business. We looked at data from 1926 to December 31, 2014. Median P/E was sorted into five quintiles, ranging from the lowest 20 percent of all month-end Median P/E readings (quintile 1) to the highest (quintile 5). The actual achieved median annualized nominal returns (before factoring in inflation) ten years later was 15.7 percent when Median P/Es were lowest (quintile 1 = lowest P/Es). Returns were just 4.3 percent annualized when Median P/Es were highest (quintile 5 = highest P/Es, or expensive hamburgers).

During an interview with a *Wall Street Journal* reporter, I tried to get this point across. I asked if it would be helpful if she picked a few dates, and I sent a summary of what the Median P/E was and what subsequent returns were achieved. I sent her this next table showing a few of her select dates along with several more. It reflects just how important starting conditions are:

### STARTING MEDIAN P/E RATIO & 10-YEAR RETURNS

| Starting Date | Starting Median P/E | 10 Yr Annualized Return |
|---|---|---|
| 12/31/1989 | 13.9 | 15.28% |
| 12/31/2000 | 20.6 | -0.48% |
| 12/31/2001 | 23.5 | 0.92% |
| 12/31/2002 | 18.8 | 4.94% |
| 02/28/2003 | 16.9 | 6.06% |
| 12/31/2003 | 21.2 | 2.17% |
| 12/31/2004 | 20.3 | 5.54% |
| 12/31/2005 | 19.0 | 5.24% |
| 12/31/2008 | 12.5 | 13.21%* |
| 02/28/2009 | 11.0 | 16.69%* |
| 12/31/2015 | 22.0 | ??? |

*Less than 10 years (through December 2015)
Source: CMG Investment Research, Ned David Research, Worldscope

As I write, we remain in quintile five. No one knows what the next year or two will bring. However, what is clear is that the stock market is richly priced and coming 10-year returns are likely to be very low.

Let's turn to Nobel Prize-winner Robert Shiller for our next set of insights.

## What Shiller P/E Tells Us about Coming Ten-Year Real Total Returns

Renowned economist and Yale professor Robert Shiller developed the cyclically adjusted price-to-earnings ratio, also called the Shiller

P/E ratio, or P/E 10. It is calculated by dividing the price by the average of ten years of earnings and adjusting it for inflation. The next chart plots each month-end Shiller P/E going back over one hundred years. As of October 2020, Shiller P/E is 29.27. Note how high the number is relative to history. And we can use it to determine future returns. Same conclusion as Median P/E: higher ratios indicate lower subsequent ten-year returns.

## S&P 500 PE Ratio

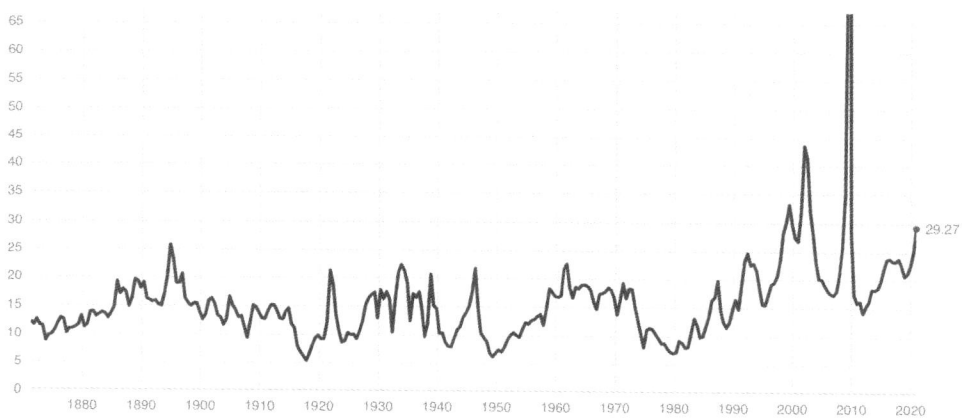

This next chart puts high Shiller P/E into perspective. Returns when starting Shiller P/E is between 20 and 48 are less than 2 percent per year the subsequent ten years.

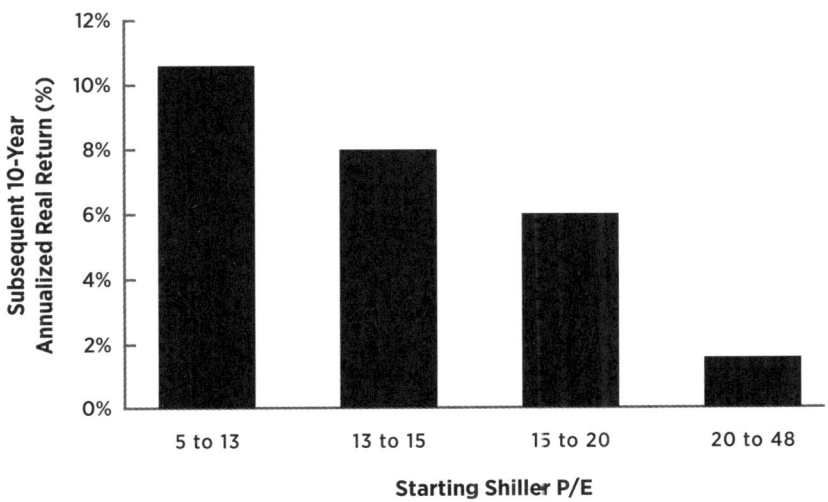

**S&P 500 INDEX RETURNS**
FROM DIFFERENT STARTING VALUATIONS

As of 3/31/15
Source: Shiller, GMO
The annualized 10-year forward real returns shown above are calculated using real price, real dividends for the S&P composite index, and cyclically adjusted P/E from the standard Shiller data source (http://www.econ.yale.edu/~shiller/data/ie_data.xls).

What is not reflected is that when valuations are highest, risk is highest. We ranked Shiller P/E into quintiles. The largest drawdown occurred when Shiller P/E was in quintile 5 (highest Shiller P/E readings)—50.9 percent versus -22.9 percent when in quintile 1 (lowest Shiller P/E readings). The average of all quintile 5 drawdowns since 1940 was 18 percent vs. an average of -4.50 percent for quintile 1. Not only are returns better when Median P/E is low, risk is also lowest. Factor that into your investment game plan.

It's not just P/E that you should keep on your radar. Let's look at a few more important valuation metrics.

## Buying Power: Stocks as a Percentage of Household Equity

Next let's look at stocks as a percentage of household assets versus the subsequent rolling S&P 500 Index total returns. The logic here is that when people are heavily invested in stocks, there is less buying power left to drive prices higher. When they are underinvested, there is more money available to boost those prices. And you'll remember from our time spent with Ray Dalio that when there are more buyers than sellers, prices are driven higher. Take a look at the next chart.

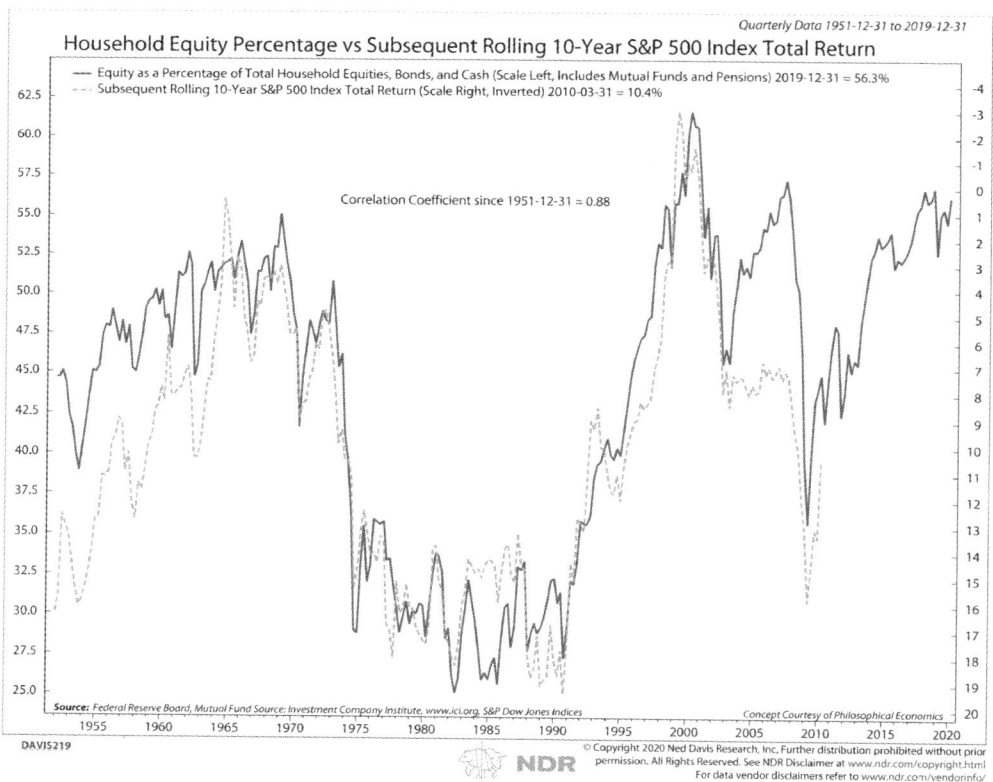

The left side of the grid plots the percentage that households have invested in equities relative to their total investment in equities, bonds, and cash. In 1982, the number was approximately 25 percent, and the subsequent ten-year S&P 500 index total return was approximately 19 percent per year. At the top of the tech bubble in 2000, households had a record high 62 percent in equities. The subsequent ten-year return was a -1.5 percent per year. At the market low point in 2009, investor ownership was forecasting a gain of 13 percent per year. It turned out to be 16 percent per year. The solid line in the chart plots the quarterly household equity percentage, and the dotted line tracks the actual return that was achieved ten years later. The two lines are highly correlated with each other, indicating that this data is too strong to be ignored. Not perfect but quite good.

When you translate this geeky data into English, it boils down to this: When investors are fully invested in stocks, there is less available capital to buy more. It's about supply and demand and available capital. Low equity percentage ownership means there is more money available to buy stocks, and the subsequent return data tells the story. Sir John Templeton said it best: "The secret to my success is I buy when everyone else is selling and I sell when everyone else is buying." This chart shows Sir John's axiom in action. I love how Ned Davis Research statistically plotted the data for our collective benefit.

As of December 31, 2019, the return forecast for the coming ten years is approximately 0.5 percent before inflation is factored in. Investors are expecting 10 percent. That is not going to happen. And 0.5 percent is just not good enough if you are a retiree looking to live off your assets after factoring in inflation. If your starting conditions resemble these, remain patient and risk focused; a better entry point is ahead.

Investors are expecting 10 percent. That is not going to happen.

## GMO's Seven-Year Real Return Forecast

Jeremy Grantham CBE is cofounder and chief investment strategist of Grantham Mayo van Otterloo & Co. (GMO), a Boston-based asset management firm. GMO has more than $118 billion in assets under management. I've been a fan of Jeremy's work for many years and have followed GMO's 7-Year Asset Class Real Return Forecasts since the late 1990s. The reason I do is that their prediction-to-outcome correlation is very high. GMO has a formula that defines their forecast approach. If you're curious about it, you can Google it. But for now, let's simply cut to the chase.

As of March 31, 2020, GMO is forecasting that US Large-Cap equities will lose 1.5 percent annually, after inflation is factored in, over the coming seven years. If you compound -1.5 percent each year for seven years, your $100,000 declines in value to $89,960.86. GMO is forecasting US Small Cap stocks will gain 1.40 percent per year, International Large-Cap companies will gain 1.90 percent per year, and emerging market stocks will gain 4.90 percent per year. They also forecast various bond markets. Unsurprisingly, they forecast that US bonds will lose 3.80 percent per year for the next seven years and that US cash money markets performing best will lose you 0.50 percent per year. Put that in your risk assessment hat. Bottom line: Not good enough.

## The Buffett Indicator: Corporate Equities-to-GDP

Back to our hamburger-loving hero. Market cap to GDP is a long-term valuation indicator that Warren Buffett popularized. Back in 2001, he remarked in a *Fortune* magazine interview that "it is probably the best single measure of where valuations stand at any given moment."[31] Market cap is calculated by taking the number of

---

31    Warren Buffett and Carol Loomis, "Warren Buffett on the Stock Market," *Fortune*. December 10, 2001.

a company's outstanding shares—IBM for example—and multiplying those shares times the current stock price. Do that for all the corporate stocks outstanding, add them all together, and you get the total market cap. Think of it as the value of all equities, and then compare that to what the United States as a country produces, or Gross Domestic Product (GDP).

This process is a stable way to see how expensively priced or inexpensively priced the stock market is at any point in time. If you look at the following chart, courtesy of Jill Mislinski at Advisor Perspectives, you can see that the Buffett Indicator says equities are priced at the second-most overvalued level since 1950. We are not getting a lot of hamburger meat for our money. It would be better to wait for opportunities similar to those that presented in 2002 and 2008–09.

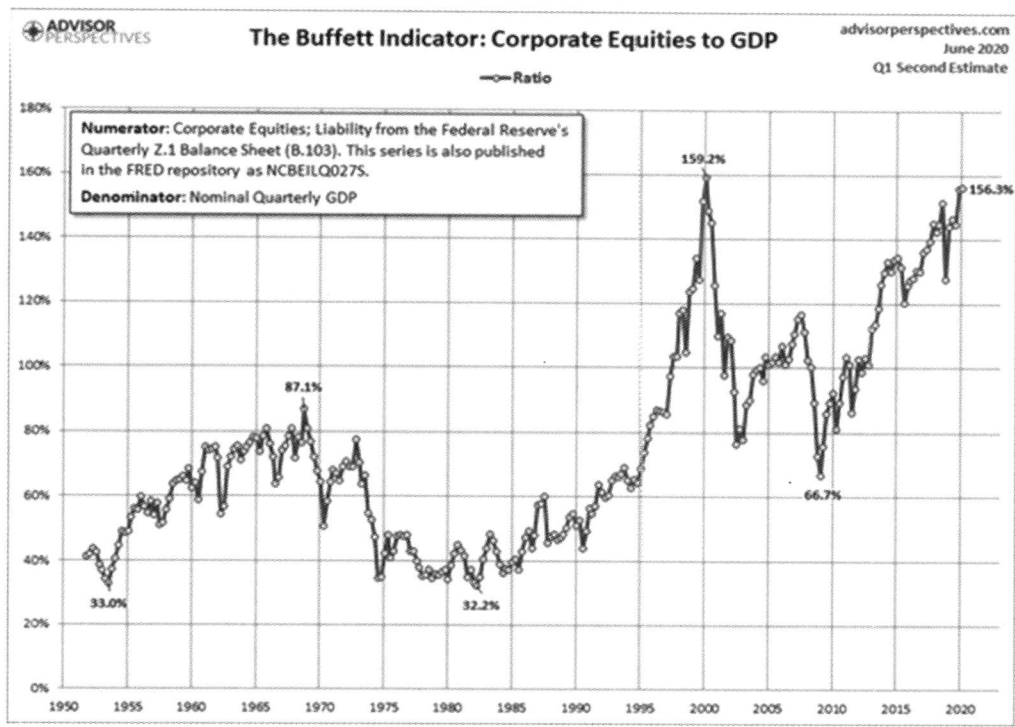

Jill also posts a similar version of the chart that looks at total stock market capitalization of the Wilshire 5000 index vs. GDP. The ratio hit 136.9 percent at the top of the tech bubble in January 2000—then a record high. It peaked at 105.2 percent in 2007, prior to the Great Financial Crisis. It currently sits at an all-time high 144.0 percent as of June 1, 2020. The point remains the same: the market is richly priced. I don't believe we'll get to the buying opportunities seen in 1982 (35 percent), 2003 (73 percent) or 2009 (57 percent) but we could. I share the charts with you in On My Radar periodically. Google CMG On My Radar to follow the free weekly blog.

## Hussman Twelve-Year Forward Returns

John Hussman, founder and president of Hussman Investment Trust, successfully predicted and managed the tech bubble and 2008–09 Great Financial Crisis. Though he remained fully hedged for a bit too long afterward, in no way should that negate his process for estimating coming returns. Hussman uses a variant of Robert Shiller's cyclically adjusted P/E (CAPE). He calls it margin-adjusted CAPE. In short, it adjusts the multiple for its embedded profit margin. This adjustment corrects for the tendency of valuation multiples to appear misleadingly low when corporate earnings are at cyclically elevated levels and to appear misleadingly high when corporate earnings are at cyclically depressed levels. The resulting measure is similar to the S&P 500 price/revenue multiple, the ratio of market capitalization to corporate gross value-added, and other measures that share a correlation near 90 percent or higher with actual subsequent ten-to-twelve-year S&P 500 total returns in market cycles across history. Ignore this process at your own peril. For the 2020 decade, margin-adjusted CAPE is telling us that returns will be -1.25 percent before inflation. His estimate for the traditional 60 percent stock, 30 percent bond, and 10 percent T-bills portfolio over the coming twelve years is for a preinflation return of just 1 percent. The culprit? The ultralow bond and T-bill yields.

Hussman explains that "the key feature of bubbles like 2000, 2007, and today is that, by the market peak, actual S&P 500 total returns over the most recent twelve-year period outpaced the return that one would have anticipated on the basis of valuations twelve years earlier. This is not an indication that valuations have failed, but rather an indication that prices are likely to do so."[32]

## Other Valuation Measures

Some may argue that I'm cherry-picking just a handful of metrics and not showing ones that predict rosier outcomes, like P/E based on Wall Street's 2019 forward estimates, for instance. Well, a detailed look across the spectrum of different valuation methods warns of an extremely overvalued stock market. Here are a few as of May 31, 2020:

- Price to Sales Ratio: 2.2 (Extremely Overvalued - Fair value is 1.0)

- Price to Book: 3.2 (Extremely Overvalued - Fair value is 1.8)

- Price to Dividend Yield: 2.0 (Extremely Overvalued – Fair value is 3.5)

- Price to Cash Flow: 15.1 (Extremely Overvalued – Fair Value is 8.9)

---

32  John Hussman, "Ground Rules of Existence," Advisor Perspectives, March 4, 2019, https://www.advisorperspectives.com/commentaries/2019/03/04/ground-rules-of-existence?utm_source=commentaries_feed&utm_medium=rss&utm_campaign=item_link.

- Price to Operating Earnings: 21.9 (Extremely Overvalued – Fair Value is 18)
- Price to Forward PE: 22.4 (Extremely Overvalued – Fair Value is 15)

Source: NDR, S&P Dow Jones Indices, S&P Capital IQ Compustat, S&P

---

There are many other valuation metrics to consider, but I'll cut to the chase: **most valuation metrics reflect an extremely overvalued, richly priced market.** Even my least-favorite valuation indicator, forward P/E, is "extremely overvalued." It's my least favorite due to the fact Wall Street analysts routinely overinflate their earnings estimates only to dial them back as earnings season nears. Those numbers start out with big expected earnings gains and almost always trend lower as the year progresses. That's why they're not my go-to.

## High Valuations Mean Higher Risk

I'd like to reiterate an important point. **Not only are returns greatest when valuations are lowest, *risk* is also lowest when valuations are low.** The reverse is true, and the weight of evidence strongly suggests, as of this writing, that valuations readings are flashing red—extremely overvalued. I'm not sure people factor the level of risk into their investment thinking, but they should. Even a retiree can overweight to stocks when prices are low, forward returns are high, and risk of loss (market volatility) is low.

With this in mind—as well as the wealth of evidence we've just covered—as of this writing, your playbook should have you playing more defense than offense. Seek growth but do so in ways that minimize your downside. Wait for the hamburgers to go down in price. Then sing the *Hallelujah* chorus along with the Buffett household—and me—when they do. The same rules apply any time: **use these valuation indicators to identify your starting conditions, for they tell you a great deal about coming five- and ten-year returns and about the level of risk—and set your investment game plan accordingly.**

I'm not sure people factor the level of risk into their investment thinking, but they should. Even a retiree can overweight to stocks when prices are low, forward returns are high, and risk of loss (market volatility) is low.

# CHAPTER 7

# Where We Sit in the Economic and Market Cycles Matters

*If we pay attention to cycles, we can come out ahead. If we study past cycles, understand their origins and import, and keep alert for the next one, we don't have to reinvent the wheel in order to understand every investment environment anew. And we have less of a chance of being blindsided by events. We can master these recurring patterns for our betterment [...] If an investor listens in this sense, he will be able to convert cycles from a wild, uncontrollable force that wreaks havoc, into a phenomenon that can be understood and taken advantage of: a vein that can be mined for significant outperformance.*

**—Howard Marks,** *Mastering the Market Cycle*

**W**hat do the current market conditions tell us about the future? We can turn to the world's leading thinkers on the subject to find out. Lucky for us, these great minds tend to gather once a year to share their insights with an audience of eager investors. The location? The Mauldin Economics Strategic Investment Conference (SIC). The conference's ultimate goal? To help investors prepare their portfolios to weather market forces with insights from those who understand them better than anyone else. And the SIC really delivers on that goal, so much so that of the more than six hundred savvy investors who attended in 2019, most had been to the conference five or more times.

The sixteenth annual conference welcomed some of the best and brightest in finance: David Rosenberg, Lacy Hunt, William White, Howard Marks, Carmen Reinhart, Mark Yusko, and Felix Zulauf, among many others. You can bet their thoughts matter. In this chapter, we'll take a look at what some of these gurus believe lies ahead, as well as their thinking on investment positioning. Keep in mind that while we're looking at a particular moment in time, much of their rationale is evergreen.

Let's kick things off with brilliant investor and cofounder of Oaktree Capital Management, Howard Marks.

## Howard Marks—A Bowl Full of Tickets

During his talk, Howard shared a powerful yet easy-to-understand analogy. He compared the investing landscape to a bowl full of tickets. The tickets represent all the potential economic factors out there—the performance of the GDP, a company, or stock in the next year, and more. Whatever is pulled from that bowl becomes the outcome investors experience.

It's in the selection of those tickets that investors' thought processes differ. Some believe there's a way to determine the ticket that will be pulled, that the process is logical and mechanical. Others think it's completely random—that the fates align to dictate the selection. Marks stressed that there are no sure things in life, and those tickets are no exception.

However, he said, that doesn't mean we can't make predictions about the outcome. Why? "Because sometimes there are more winning tickets in the bowl than losing tickets, sometimes there are more losing tickets in the bowl than winners, and an exceptional investor is someone who has an above average awareness of the tickets in the bowl, even if he doesn't know what the outcome is going to be."[33] Thus, it goes almost without saying that "you should invest more when the tickets in the bowl are in your favor. You should invest less when the tickets are against your favor."[34]

How do you know the ratio of winners to losers in the bowl? The mix largely depends on where we are in the cycle. As of this writing, and Marks's explanation, we're sitting late in the cycle. He added, "I think of things as being cheap, fair, or rich. And today, broadly speaking, there is nothing cheap." He explained that the question then becomes, *What is least overpriced?* The least worst, in other words. "Then," he continued, "you have to say, given the fact that the economic recovery is the longest in history and the bull market is the longest in history and the world is leveraged and there are all these cosmic things going on, the results of which are unpredictable, in investing in the medium term you should ask yourself if you want to be on offense or defense. We sit late in the cycle. I think that the

---

33   Howard Marks, "Generation-Changing Debt" (Panel at Mauldin Economics Strategic Investment Conference, Dallas, May 16, 2019).

34   Ibid.

probability of high returns is low and the probability of low returns is high."[35] When circumstances mirror these conditions, it's time to play more defense.

## Lacy Hunt

What does internationally renowned economist Dr. Lacy Hunt of Hoisington Investment Management Company think? With the conditions as they are, he sees Fed Funds rates reaching 0 percent. He worries that we'll be stuck in a quagmire with those rates and that the yield curve will be a lot flatter. He foresees things getting ugly economically, with the ten-year declining to 1 percent and the thirty-year bottoming at a yield of 2 percent.

What's behind his thinking? Two theorems. The first is that federal debt accelerations ultimately lead to lower, not higher, interest rates. He explained, "debt-funded traditional fiscal stimulus is extremely fleeting when debt levels are already inordinately high. Thus, additional and large deficits provide only transitory gains in economic activity, which are quickly followed by weaker business conditions. With slower economic growth and inflation, longer-term rates inevitably fall."[36] It's a mouthful, but ultimately, the message is clear: that rate drop is unavoidable.

The second theorem states, "Monetary decelerations eventually lead to lower, not higher, interest rates, as originally theorized by economist Milton Friedman. As debt productivity falls, the velocity of money declines, making monetary policy increasingly asymmetric (one sided) and ineffectual as an instrument of monetary

---

35  Ibid.

36  Lacy Hunt, "Two Theorems for Evaluating Monetary Effects on Interest Rates" (Presented to Mauldin Economics Strategic Investment Conference, Dallas, May 14, 2019).

acceleration."[37] Remember those levers Dalio described earlier? Hunt says they're about to be out of order—and unable to help us out of this mess.

What kind of strategy does Hunt suggest under these circumstances? Based on his belief that we have not yet seen the bottom of the declining rate cycle, he favors investing in long-term government bonds.

## David Rosenberg

How about Rosenberg Research's founder, chief economist, and strategist David Rosenberg, whom you may know by his twitter handle, @EconguyRosie? Rosie argues that recession is coming, rates are heading lower, and we will move toward an even more unconventional Fed policy. With rates heading lower, he, too, is bullish on Treasury notes and bonds over the coming twelve months. He also likes quality dividend payers and going long on volatility. For nongeeks, that's a bet that volatility will pick up to the downside (it will get very bumpy). How do you play that for profit? Rosie says you can invest in the VIX Index, which measures thirty-day expected volatility of the stock market based on S&P 500 prices. As my dad would say, that's "a play that's not for the faint of heart."

In the end, he sees a future "debt jubilee," where debt is somehow monetized, followed by inflation.

The bottom line according to Rosie? Recession is coming sooner than most believe. Rates are headed lower. Strategy-wise, he likes more defensive

> Recession is coming sooner than most believe.

---

37   Ibid.

stocks like high dividend payers, long-term treasury bonds, and an active approach to trading.

## William R. White

For the Canadian economist and former chairman of the Economic and Development Review Committee at the Bank for International Settlements (BIS), the central bankers' central bank, it's all about flaws. Bill says the central bankers' policies are fundamentally flawed. He believes their flawed theory has led to flawed policy, both before and after the last crisis, and that flawed policy will usher in the next one. "We've had a noninflationary boom," he said, and in the next crisis, he predicts we are going to have a "debt-deflationary bust, but what that might morph into is high inflation or even hyperinflation."[38]

A major issue? The Fed's (and other central bankers') capacity to respond is now significantly reduced.

Last time, interest rates were much higher. Right now, they're pretty close to zero in most places and actually negative in many others. The balance sheets are also much larger: in the United States, the Fed's balance sheet is 20 percent of GDP; in Europe, the ECP is 40 percent of GDP; and in Japan, the BOJ is 100 percent of GDP. While there may still be room to adjust, there's far less of it due to the degree to which sovereign debt ratios in the advanced countries have ballooned.

Moreover, he explained that the Fed's "crisis-resolution tools are inadequate [this time around] … Dodd-Frank has got six separate provisions in it that will prevent the Fed from doing next time what

---

38  William R. White, Presentation to Mauldin Economics Strategic Investment Conference, Dallas, May 14, 2019.

they did the last time."[39]

He tells those thinking their way through the outcome he sees, with deflation occurring first, followed by inflation, "In the end the only way out of this mess is inflation." White advised the audience to put a lot more emphasis on what's happening geopolitically, since that's where the action is going to be taking place. His sign off? "Good luck. You're probably going to need it."[40]

## Felix Zulauf

Felix Zulauf is the owner and president of Switzerland-based Zulauf Asset Management and former global strategist at the largest bank in Switzerland. Zulauf began his presentation by explaining his process. "When I look at markets," he said, "I first start to create a long-term big picture. I look at structural trends in economics, in demographics, in politics, etc., etc. And then I try to analyze the business cycle and where we sit in the cycle."[41]

He stated that demographics are what's missing from other econometric models—they don't take that key factor into account and adapt accordingly. Zulauf shared a numerical snapshot of demographics past, present, and future: The number of zero to sixty-four-year-olds in OECD-member countries, plus China, Brazil, and Russia, grew by 25 million every year from the 1950s to the 1970s. But since then, that number has been declining. It was down to 14 million in 2008, the last time we had a crisis. Last year, there was zero growth. 2019 was the first year growth was negative, at -1.7 million.

39    Ibid.

40    Ibid.

41    Felix Zulauf, Presentation to Mauldin Economics Strategic Investment Conference, Dallas, May 14, 2019.

It is estimated to drop to -12 million by the year 2030 and stay there until the early 2040s.

Because economic growth (GDP) equals productivity times population growth (aka demographics), growth will be low for a longer period of time. That's a real problem, since our economic system is built on growth. It's a necessary factor for the system's survival. When growth is stagnant, there ends up being a fight for market share, and that fight shows up in trade wars. One player starts cheating with currency manipulation so their products cost less, another player responds, and finally, tariffs are imposed. That's where we are today. You see the rising conflicts in trade and geopolitics, and the issue compounds when a dominating power is challenged by a rising economic power with a strong military (that's the United States and China). Over the last five hundred years, there have been sixteen such cases, twelve of which ended in outright war. That's the kind of environment we are moving into, and Zulauf predicts that it will only get worse over the next ten years.

Then we come to the business cycle. The tariff and trade problems are just compounding the global slowdown we're seeing, which is a result of overtightening in the United States and China—the world's two largest economies—and it's classic. And Europe is heavily dependent on China, with half its growth over the last ten years coming from China, both directly and indirectly. The global business slowdown will eventually have an impact on markets.

Unfortunately, Zulauf thinks the Fed and global central bankers just don't understand markets and remain married to their flawed economic models. As a result, they make mistakes at critical junctures. What does that mean for the future? He thinks the central banks will become even more powerful—not in terms of the effect they have on the economy but the effect they have on the markets.

And though he believes they'll continue to print money, current conditions will prohibit that money from stimulating growth—there is just too much debt. Instead, that money will inflate asset prices. And ultimately, those central bankers will have widened the rift between the haves and the have-nots. This is evident today.

What does all of that translate to in terms of market movement? He sees big swings in the equity market over the next ten years, with no net gain in price. Those who buy and hold will earn, at best, the dividend yield. Rallies will be followed by large declines—the central bankers will respond aggressively, the market will bottom, and then rally again. He, like Hunt, White, Rosenberg and me, believes the Fed Funds rate could be at 0 percent. Then what? he asks. We're moving from a "passive investor's market" to a "trader's market."

## Markets Cycle

*Cycles are inevitable.*
*Every once in a while, an up- or down-leg goes*
*on for a long time and/or to a great extreme, and*
*people start to say "this time it's different."*
### —Howard Marks

The point of my global weekly musing, On My Radar, is to simply take a step back and do our best to identify where we sit in the economic and market cycles. In his must-read book *Mastering the Market Cycle*, Howard Marks shared the simple chart I shared with you in Chapter 4. Here it is again with my notations: "We are here" and "We'd be better off here":

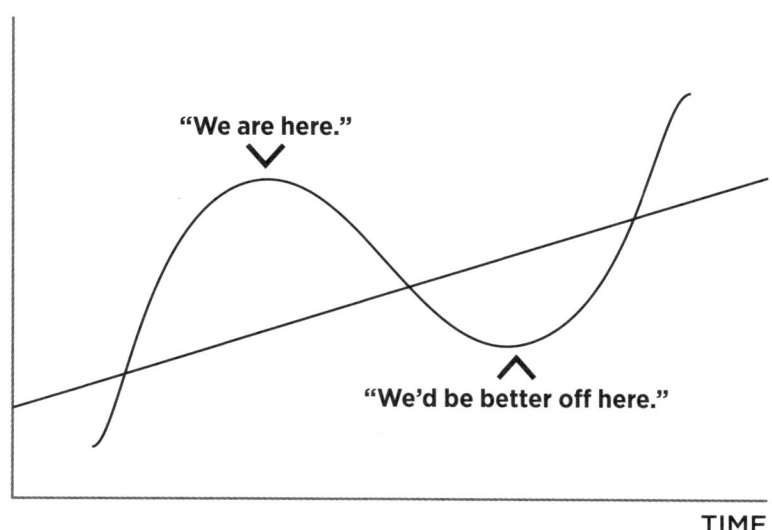

"We are here."

"We'd be better off here."

TIME

While there are peaks and valleys along the way, the long-term growth line is moving up. I'm convinced that businesses will experience relatively consistent growth over time. The problem is that, as we discussed, investors push prices above that long-term growth trend. This creates market risk, which is different from business risk. Better portfolio diversification can help you deal with business-related risks. That will help you grow your wealth, but you've also got to find ways to defend it from market risks.

> While there are peaks and valleys along the way, the long-term growth line is moving up.

That steady line across the middle follows a growth rate of 10.1 percent over a long period of time. At least, that is what the S&P 500 cap-weighted index has produced over a very long time horizon. As such, it's a good guess as to how much gain per year you can expect from the stock market over a long-term time horizon. But depending on where we sit in the cycle, investors may find themselves facing some real issues. If prices are bid up way above that long-term trend, your market risk is high. Prices will always revert back to trend and almost always drop down below the long-term growth trend (the straight line in the middle of that simple chart). This is due to investor psychology. It's just the way it is, and thirty-six years of experience working with investors tells me, unfortunately, it won't ever change.

If we convert the preceding chart into a real-life chart, it looks like the following.

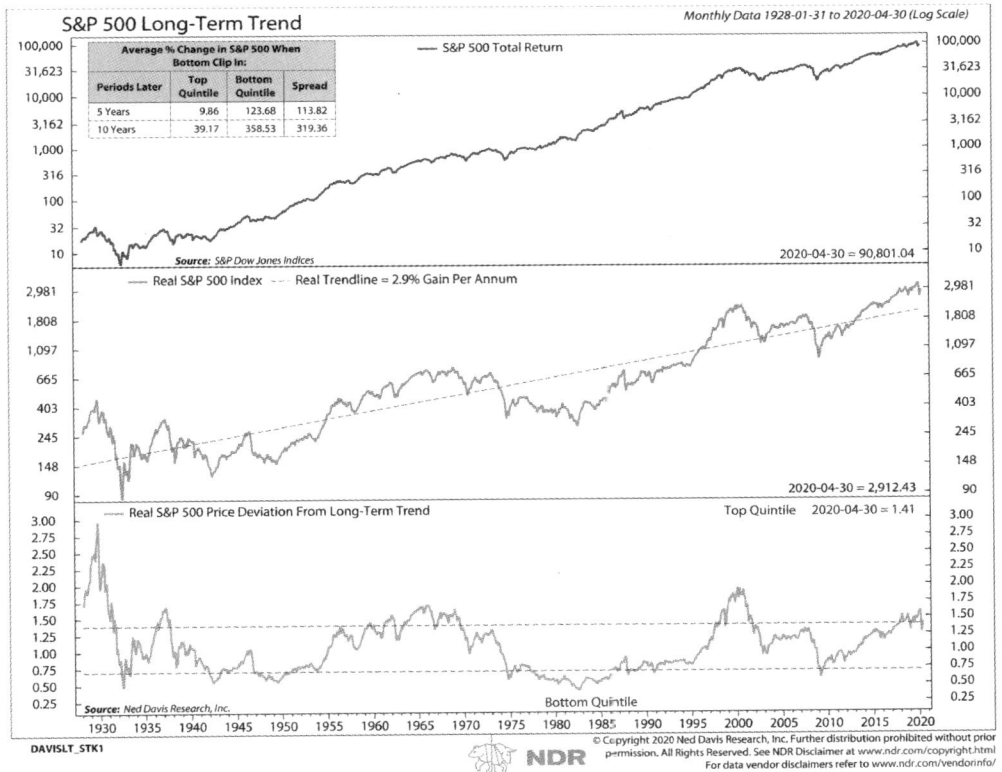

Here is how you read it:

Focus in on the middle section. The dotted line is like the diagonal growth line in the chart above. Note how the market price trend of the S&P 500 index, the line in the middle section of the chart, moves above and below the long-term trend line (dotted line).

The bottom section measures the price deviation from the trend, and the data box in the upper left shows us the achieved returns based on starting conditions (note that when price moved well above its long-term growth trend, the gain in the S&P 500 index in the subsequent five- and ten-year periods was low, and when it was below trend, subsequent returns were highest). Bottom line: Expect low five- and ten-year returns. Not good.

Knowing where we are in the cycle can help you shape your investment return odds. The timing of all dislocations remains largely elusive, but you can measure the probability of your return and the degree of risk you are taking. Simple rule: Play offense when you are at or below trend. Play defense when far above it. And don't ever let it stress you out.

Early cycle, midcycle, or late cycle? As we enter the 2020s, the collective wisdom from these seasoned investment minds and the simple understanding of price movement relative to long-term trend growth suggest we sit late cycle.

Further, as you'll see next, understanding what equity valuation levels tell you about coming future returns can aid you in adapting your investment strategy as necessary.

## The Best Return Indicator: Total Stock Market Cap vs. Nominal Gross Domestic Income

Having the chance to hear from investing greats—and to share those insights with you—helps me think about and challenge my own perspective on the economy, interest rates, and the stock market.

We've already talked at length about my belief that valuations are crucial in terms of determining what returns are likely to be over the coming ten years. Zulauf sees wide swings in the market, both on the upside and the downside, but predicts that we'll end up in the same place we are today ten years from now. No price appreciation, with the best case being that investors earn the current dividend yield of 1.82 percent. I think that's about right. Let's talk about why.

In Chapter 6, we reviewed Warren Buffett's favorite valuation chart, which compares the total value of the stock market to Nominal Gross Domestic Product (GDP). It showed the market at the second-most overvalued level since 1950. A variant of this measure looks at the Stock Market Capitalization vs. National Gross Domestic Income. Think of Gross Domestic Income as what we collectively earn. When stock prices go up, the collective value of the market goes up, and when you compare it to our collective income, you get a ratio to determine if prices got ahead of themselves (overvalued) or are cheap relative to our incomes (undervalued). If your company's is worth $2.51 million and your income is $1 million, your stock market cap vs. your income is 151.69 percent.

Ned David Research (NDR) tested the data back to 1925 and organized the ratio of stock market value to income into five quintiles (most overvalued to undervalued). The results are detailed in the next chart. Looking at subsequent returns the coming one-, three-, five-, seven-, nine- and eleven-year return data from 1925 to April 2020 paints a challenging investor-return picture for the period ahead. The dotted line in the middle section is the long-term trend. The "Top Quintile" returns tell us returns are likely to be negative over the coming nine years. Eleven years from now, if the actual historical numbers prove similar, $100,000 will grow to just $101,410 before inflation.

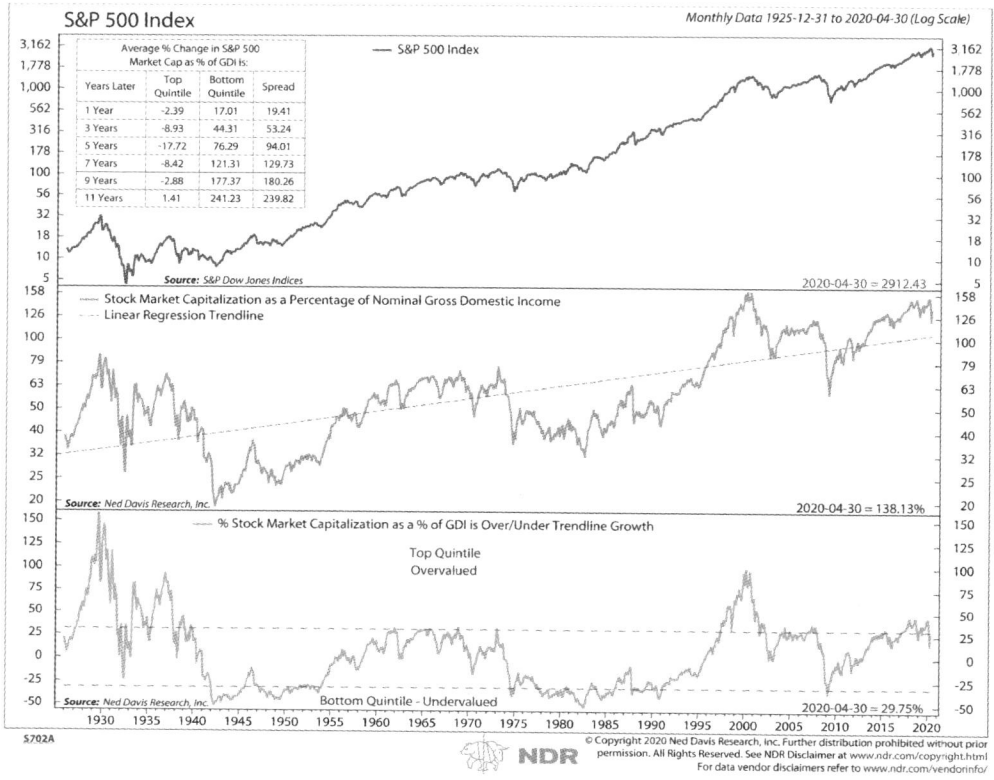

S&P 500 Index — Monthly Data 1925-12-31 to 2020-04-30 (Log Scale)

Average % Change in S&P 500 Market Cap as % of GDI is:

| Years Later | Top Quintile | Bottom Quintile | Spread |
|---|---|---|---|
| 1 Year | -2.39 | 17.01 | 19.41 |
| 3 Years | -8.93 | 44.31 | 53.24 |
| 5 Years | -17.72 | 76.29 | 94.01 |
| 7 Years | -8.42 | 121.31 | 129.73 |
| 9 Years | -2.88 | 177.37 | 180.26 |
| 11 Years | 1.41 | 241.23 | 239.82 |

Source: S&P Dow Jones Indices

2020-04-30 = 2912.43

Stock Market Capitalization as a Percentage of Nominal Gross Domestic Income
Linear Regression Trendline

Source: Ned Davis Research, Inc.

2020-04-30 = 138.13%

% Stock Market Capitalization as a % of GDI is Over/Under Trendline Growth

Top Quintile Overvalued

Source: Ned Davis Research, Inc.

Bottom Quintile - Undervalued

2020-04-30 = 29.75%

S702A

© Copyright 2020 Ned Davis Research, Inc. Further distribution prohibited without prior permission. All Rights Reserved. See NDR Disclaimer at www.ndr.com/copyright.html
For data vendor disclaimers refer to www.ndr.com/vendorinfo/

Lastly, compare the returns that were achieved when your starting condition was in the bottom quintile. I'm suggesting patience until the valuations revert back to the long-term trend (i.e., the dotted linear regression trendline in the middle section of the chart). At that point, I believe it is reasonable to expect 10.1 percent annualized returns from your S&P 500 large-cap equity-weighted index fund or ETF. That's the long-term return we previously discussed.

I want to make an important point. Just because our current starting position is one of low to negative five- and ten-year returns, that doesn't mean that is what you need to earn. It simply indicates that you should defend your wealth now so you are in a position to take advantage of the higher returns the next market dislocation will create.

NDR said that no indicator they have tested has done a better job showing subsequent returns. We should take note. The goal, of course, is to grow and defend your wealth. This indicator is telling us to play more defense than offense. Put in place and stick to a disciplined stop-loss risk-management game plan. More on how to do that in Chapter 9. Let's cover some concluding thoughts on the importance of understanding economic and market cycles.

## The Long-Term Debt Cycle Revisited

Debt has been used to fuel growth but now sits at levels that impede it. Debt itself is at the core of the global economic illness. If your brother-in-law accumulates too much debt, he has less income to spend on new things. More of his money must go toward paying back what he borrowed. His personal economy slows, and his stress level rises. He's desperate to figure out how to escape his mess. For countries, creditable academic research says stress begins when the debt-to-income ratio exceeds 90 percent.

We took a look at the global landscape in Chapter 2, "How the Economic Machine Works." Debt-GDP is 327.3 percent in the United States, 457.5 percent in the Eurozone, 595.5 percent in Japan, 515.7 percent in France, 460.3 percent in the United Kingdom, and 291.9 percent in Germany.

If 90 percent is that stress threshold, what on God's green earth does 325.8 percent in the United States, 457.7 percent in the Eurozone, or 595.8 percent in Japan do to us?

Central bankers have driven rates to levels seen in the 1930s, the peak in the last long-term debt cycle. And in some parts of the developed world, rates are negative. When someone tells you something has never happened before, the truth is it likely has—just not in that person's lifetime. However, never before in history have we seen government debts yielding less than zero. This is truly uncharted territory.

> When someone tells you something has never happened before, the truth is it likely has—just not in that person's lifetime. However, never before in history have we seen government debts yielding less than zero. This is truly uncharted territory.

Overbought, overvalued, overleveraged late-cycle conditions, like the ones we are facing at this writing, warn us that something serious is brewing. Simply, be aware and prepared. It takes patience because it is impossible to know the magnitude and timing of the next recession. Businesses will face challenges, especially those most overleveraged in debt. No one knows how quickly central bankers and policy makers will respond. No one knows! It's probable that central bankers will be first to the rescue, but one has to question how effective they can be. Much of the ammo has been spent. Divided politicians? I'm less confident. As we discussed in Chapter 3, long-term debt cycles are most challenging. That's where we find ourselves today. Few of us have seen this movie before, but it's been made. Just know #RiskHappensFast. Keep your lights on.

## The End Game

We all want growth and prosperity. To achieve it, legislators and central bankers around the globe will need to figure out how to solve for the challenging period ahead. It's complicated, and we'll get through it. But it will take time, political will, and collaboration.

Ultimately, we'll need to come together to determine how to burn the debt. As investors, we'll need to recognize that, along the way, we must adapt.

The risk of all of this global financial misbehavior is inflation. As Bill White stated in his presentation at the Mauldin Strategic Investment Conference, the Fed's "crisis-resolution tools are inadequate [this time around]." He advised you (and me) to think through the implications of the outcome he sees: deflation first, then inflation. Let his conclusion stick with you: "In the end, the only way out of this mess is inflation."[42]

But the question remains: What do you do about it?

Howard Marks said it best: "If an investor listens in this sense, he will be able to convert cycles from a wild, uncontrollable force that wreaks havoc, into a phenomenon that can be understood and taken advantage of: a vein that can be mined for significant outperformance."[43]

Thankfully, by knowing that markets do indeed cycle, you can adapt. Let's look at a few ideas that can help you gain equity market exposure in a healthier way and then talk about how to risk-manage your way through the corrective phases of market cycles.

> **By knowing that markets do indeed cycle, you can adapt.**

---

42   White, 2019.

43   Marks, Howard. *Mastering the Market Cycle: Getting the Odds on Your Side.* New York. Houghton Mifflin Harcourt, 2018.

# CHAPTER 8

# Diversification Matters

U nderstanding market cycles is key to your success, allowing you to adapt and remain mindful of market risks, all while seeking growth. We'll next look at a better way to own exposure to equities, as well as a few ways to manage market risks, but first, let me tell you a little story.

Nearly twenty years ago, I met my dear friend Mark Finn. Mark is a consultant to major pension plans and in earlier years ran the State of Virginia's pension system. To be frank, he is one of the smartest investors I know.

In 2006, Mark called me to tell me that he had formed a venture capital fund and asked me if I would be interested in it. "Mark," I said, "I'll invest in anything you touch."

Mark established the venture fund in partnership with an individual named Rory Riggs. Riggs came from the biotechnology space, where he cofounded a company called Royalty Pharma with a revolutionary concept: rather than owning shares in the companies that produced certain drugs, you would share in the revenue stream from future pharmaceutical drug sales. Royalty Pharma is now a multi-billion-dollar fund—the largest of its kind. When you're that big, you see a lot of investment opportunities. Some of the opportunities Riggs and his team were seeing weren't mature enough for Royalty Pharma, but they still had real potential. So Finn and Riggs created a venture fund for smaller, earlier-stage opportunities. That's the fund Mark had called to ask me about, and I'm fortunate to have invested in it.

In 2009, Mark called me again. "I've been talking to someone, and I think he's got something special," Mark said. "I think he might win the Nobel Prize for this someday." We agreed to talk about it over a round of golf.

"I'm under an NDA," Mark began, "so I can't tell you the whole story, but I can share the basics. Imagine a better way to index—kind of like what Rob Arnott did with smart beta." Arnott fundamentally weighted the same five hundred stocks that make up the S&P 500 capitalized-weighted funds and ETFs, which later became known as a new asset category called smart beta. Equally weighting a basket of stocks, like fundamental weight, produces better return and risk statistics over time. "It's a different weighting methodology that really gets at the root of what businesses do and their potential," Mark said.

Around the fourth hole, he gave me a few more details about the mysterious guy whose idea we had been discussing. "He came from this big pharmaceutical fund," he said.

I looked at him, "Mark, are you talking about Rory?" I asked.

"Yeah. How do you know Rory?"

"I'm invested in your venture capital fund!" I replied. "So tell me more about what this biotech guy is doing in finance."

Full disclosure: I've been an advisor to the company Rory formed to bring his high-potential idea, Syntax, to life since 2009. As you read on, please be aware that conflict of interest exists.

For years, Rory and his team have coded the individual risk attributes of 8,500 publicly traded companies. They built a database that allows for a deeper understanding of the related business risks companies have. By understanding the similar risk profiles that companies have, one can create better diversification; the depth of programming Rory and his team has done allows for a clear picture of the related business risks that exist across companies. In short, over a full market cycle, owning the same five hundred stocks, or any broad basket of stocks, fundamental-weight and equal-weight indices do better than traditional cap-weighted indices, and Syntax's weighting mythology does even better. Again, each owns the *exact same* stocks. I believe that what Rory and his team are doing is truly innovative and captures what we've been after in this business for years: real beta.

Investors are always seeking tools that can help us do better. By more accurately identifying related business risks, I believe Syntax's mythology allows investors to own the market in the broadest, most balanced way possible. Before we talk about how it works, let's talk about why diversification and finding a better way to achieve it—like the one Syntax offers—is so important.

## The Problem with Cap-Weighted Indices

There are numerous investment products out there that aim to meet investors' needs: stocks, bonds, index funds, exchange-traded funds (ETFs), and more. A significant amount of investor capital is concentrated in cap-weighted indices. Cap-weighted indices were designed to provide a benchmark to which institutional investors could compare performance of their active managers. The financial industry has adopted cap-weighted as the proxy for market beta (the return the market gives you). No one envisioned these indices would become investable products, yet that's what happened. Let's look at some numbers.

The total US stock market is approximately $31 trillion, of which $11.7 trillion is benchmarked to S&P Dow Jones indices. Of that, $9.9 trillion is indexed or benchmarked to the S&P 500; $3.4 trillion is in index-based mutual funds and ETF products; and $639 billion is in the three largest S&P 500 Index ETFs: "SPY," the S&P 500 ticker from State Street SPDR; "IVV," the iShares S&P 500 Index; and "VOO," the Vanguard S&P 500 ETF.[44]

In global markets, everyone has adapted this cap-weighted methodology as well. But there is a problem, and most don't know it exists. One of the challenges with cap-weighted indices is that, by rule, the larger the value of a company (determined by multiplying its outstanding shares times its market price) becomes, the larger the weighting the stock gets within an index. If everyone piles into technology stocks, they drive the price of those stocks higher, and by rule, technology stocks get a higher weighting within the index. The result? Overconcentration and increased risk. That's not a bad thing if the market is going up and tech is on fire. But it's extremely detrimental when things fall apart, because it means you've overconcentrated in the places that will sustain the most damage.

For example, in 1999, technology stocks became over 46.5 percent of the S&P 500 index. Prior to the great tech bubble, technology exposure was 17 percent. Most sectors did okay, but the overconcentration in technology brought cap-weighted indices—and many

---

44  S&P Dow Jones Indices, Ned Davis Research, Bank of International Settlements, https://www.spglobal.com/en/capabilities/benchmarks, https://us.spindices.com/indices/equity/sp-500.

investors—down. As of May 31, 2020, technology, by rule, represents 45 percent of the cap-weighted S&P 500 index. And of the entire S&P 500, just six stocks (Facebook, Amazon, Apple, Microsoft, Netflix and Google) represent 21 percent of the S&P 500 index.[45] Time after time, we end up with overweighting mismatches. That's a problem.

In 2000, information tools (IT) and information were weighted at 29 and 17.5 percent, respectively. Then, technology represented 46.5 percent of the cap-weighted S&P 500 index. A year later, IT was down 63.3 percent, and information was down 30.9 percent. Three years later, they were down 39.2 percent and 24.8 percent. All the pain came from those two technology sectors. They fell apart—and badly so. But most of the market was not down. If you owned the Syntax Stratified Large Cap index, you would have actually been up 10 percent per year rather than down 5 percent per year owning the S&P 500 index from March 31, 2000 to March 31, 2005. That's a very big difference. Why does this happen? We can chalk it up to investor behavior. Investors herd into and bid up the share price of popular stocks, and by rule, the S&P 500 index overweights various stock types. In 2000, it was technology stocks. In 2008, the S&P 500 index overweighted financial stocks. Both instances were caused by the same herding misbehavior. Syntax found that their weighting process outperforms the S&P 500 in 79 percent of down markets by an average of 8.8 percent, outperforms in 60 percent of up markets by an average of 2 percent, and outperforms in 63 percent of all markets by an average of 3.2 percent.[46]

---

45   S&P Dow Jones Indices as of May 31, 2020.

46   Trailing twelve-month total return, December 20, 1991–June 30, 2019. Performance does not reflect fees or implementation costs, as an investor cannot directly invest in an index. Please see important disclaimers regarding back-tested data prior to inception on December 27, 2016. Source: S&P Dow Jones Indices, Syntax.

Just ask the late financial historian and economist Peter Bernstein. He knew how easy it is to get overconfident and how dangerous that can be. "The riskiest moment is when you're right. That's when you're in the most trouble, because you tend to overstay the good decisions. Once you've been right for long enough, you don't even *consider* reducing your winning positions. They feel so good, you can't even face that. As incredible as it sounds, that makes you comfortable with *not being diversified.* So, in many ways, it's better not to be so right. That's what diversification is for. It's an explicit recognition of ignorance."[47]

> The riskiest moment is when you're right. That's when you're in the most trouble, because you tend to overstay the good decisions. Once you've been right for long enough, you don't even *consider* reducing your winning positions.

The lack of diversification has a significant impact, in more ways than one. Ideally, those invested in stocks should get a higher return than if they were to invest in bonds. Think about it: corporations are borrowing money in hopes of attaining a particular growth outcome that is higher than the rate at which they're borrowing. Boards are driving leadership teams. Leadership teams are driving management teams. Managers are driving their staff to achieve a desired goal.

With all of that considered, equity should provide a fairly consistent return premium over fixed income, but due to the overcon-

---

47    Jason Zweig, "Peter Bernstein Interview: He May Know More About Investing Than Anyone Alive" *Money*, October 15, 2004, https://money.cnn.com/2004/10/11/markets/benstein_bonus_0411/index.htm.

centration that happens in cap-weighted indices, that's not necessarily the case.

So how do you achieve diversification when investor behavior limits it in cap-weighted funds? Rory Riggs recognized this issue and set out to address it.

## A Better Way

Combining his knack for both business and science with a clear vision, Rory determined that we could find a better answer by applying a new strategy. The idea came from a key concept in health care. In clinical trials, physicians and researchers use a standard set of genetic attributes to randomly group patient populations. Doing so prevents imbalances between treatment groups (e.g., an overrepresentation of people with a specific trait) and helps ensure that any results derived from a trial accurately represent the outcomes that would be achieved with members of the broader population. Rory realized he could apply a similar logic to businesses. He could actually code various business traits. If he could account for those traits, he could derive better diversification.

So he founded a company that would do just that: Syntax. He hired a team, and together, they created a common language to identify the components that compose a business's DNA. Rather than specific genetic markers—the building blocks of humanity—the technology they developed codes the attributes of what a company does and how its products are sourced and sold. From component parts to distribution pathways, the people and organizations who use certain products, how much of a company's products are sold to whom (businesses, consumers, governments, etc.) where and at what cost—Syntax tracked it down and coded it all.

With the attributes that make up a company clearly defined, investors can clearly identify the *related business risk* that exists between the individual companies in their portfolio, in their broad index and sector funds, and across their active portfolio managers. Across your various portfolios, mutual funds and money managers, you can now see if you are as diversified as you might think.

Related business risk is the concept that companies that share similar characteristics and circumstances—producing the same types of products, selling to the same groups of people, or operating in the same value chain—also share the same risks. For example, many companies in the agricultural industry may suffer if there is a severe drought or trade conflict. Or widespread worker strikes might disrupt the productivity of multiple shipping businesses.

All this information serves a greater purpose: if an investor can understand how various businesses' risks overlap with other companies' risks, they can balance those risks and create better diversification. That's where the Syntax solution comes into play.

## How You Combine Various Risks Matters!

With this information, it's possible to take almost any combination of stocks—the Russell 2000, the Wilshire 5000, the Dow Jones—anything—and determine how to diversify based on business-risk attributions rather than the size of a company.

That's what Syntax did. The team applied their technology to eighteen benchmark indices, including the S&P 500, S&P MidCap 300, MSCI EAFE, Russell 1000, and Wilshire 5000, and reweighted them, creating equal exposure across every business risk category. The outcome: the Syntax Stratified-Weight Indices have outperformed cap-weighted indices, equal-weighted indices, and fundamental-weighted indices since December 20, 1991. Because stratified indices are better diversified, the impact of related business risk correlations is reduced.

We looked at the tech bubble data above. It's a somewhat similar story for the Great Financial Crisis. Just prior to the crisis, financial stocks composed 21.7 percent of the S&P 500—and just 12.5 percent of the pie in the Strati-

> **Because stratified indices are better diversified, the impact of related business risk correlations is reduced.**

fied LargeCap Index. The difference in return? Negative 1.6 percent annually for the S&P 500 versus a positive 3.7 percent annually for Stratified LargeCap from December 31, 2006, to December 31, 2011. Healthier weighting makes all the difference.

The following chart shows that diversifying related business risk enhances returns overall. The chart compares the performance of Syntax Stratified LargeCap, the S&P 500 Equal Weight, FTSE RAFI US 1000, NYSE Select Sector Equal Weight, S&P 500 Value, and the S&P 500. The Syntax Stratified LargeCap Index holds the exact same securities that are held in each of the indices. S&P Dow Jones Indices is the calculation agent for the Syntax Stratified LargeCap index, the S&P 500, the S&P 500 Value, the S&P 500 Equal Weight, and the S&P 500 Revenue-Weighted indices using the same pricing, corporate action treatment, and calculation methodology. Again, the only difference is the weights.

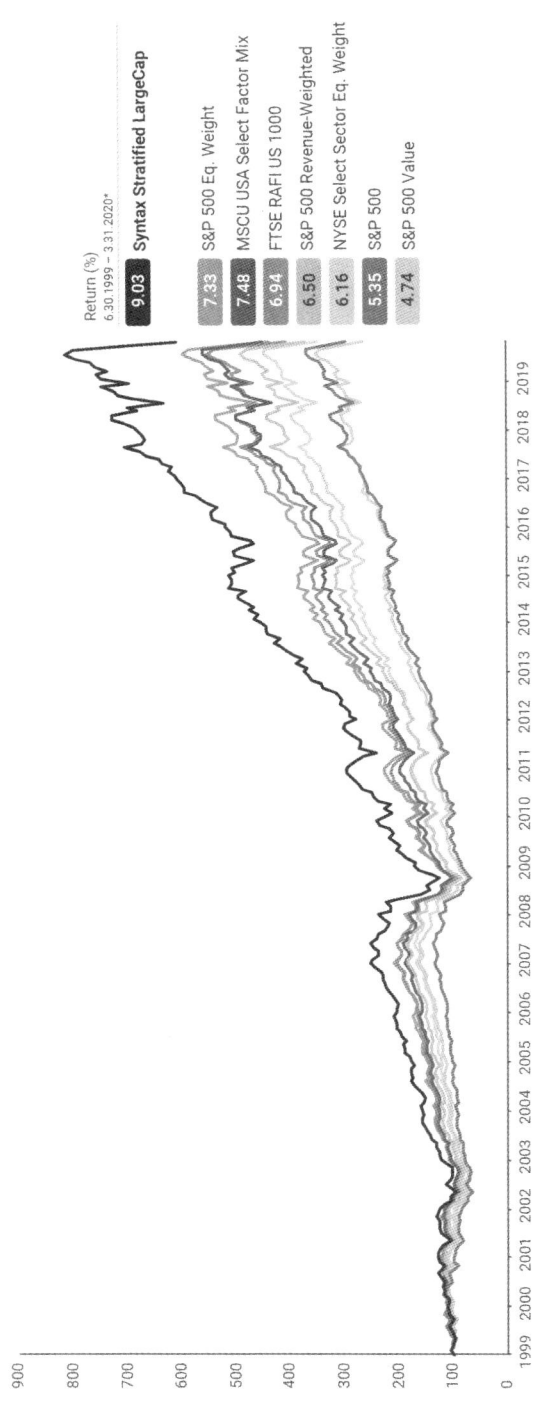

Return (%)
6.30.1999 – 3.31.2020*

| | |
|---|---|
| 9.03 | **Syntax Stratified LargeCap** |
| 7.33 | S&P 500 Eq. Weight |
| 7.48 | MSCU USA Select Factor Mix |
| 6.94 | FTSE RAFI US 1000 |
| 6.50 | S&P 500 Revenue-Weighted |
| 6.16 | NYSE Select Sector Eq. Weight |
| 5.35 | S&P 500 |
| 4.74 | S&P 500 Value |

Source: Syntax

There are a number of research papers available at www.Syntax. us. The process is not perfect, nor are the equal weighted and cap-weighted methodologies. There are times when cap-weight will out-perform, especially during periods when just a few names account for the majority of the performance. The bottom line here? Diversifica-tion can make a tremendous difference in an investor's outcomes. It *really* matters.

But our exploration of our question, *What do you do about it?* doesn't end here. There's more you can do to make sure you stay in the game. It's also about adopting a balanced, effective approach, one that isn't swayed by emotions or bad behavior (whether yours or other investors').

Remember the great Paul Tudor Jones's tuition-saving advice to his students—that all they had to do to avoid the burden of financing a business school education was put a two-hundred-day stop-loss moving average on everything they owned? That insight is valuable because it keeps you in the game by limiting your downside loss.

Trend following capitalizes on that idea. It is a process by which investors are able to risk-manage their exposures. There are multiple ways to do it, but the simple principle behind it is that by keeping your principal intact—by avoiding the really big mistakes—you stay in the game. Next, we'll talk more about trend following as well as some additional ideas you can utilize to avoid the 30 percent to 50 percent declines that tend to occur once or twice every decade.

# CHAPTER 9

# Adapt to Succeed—How to Grow and Defend Your Wealth

There is a difference between business risk and market risk. In the previous chapter, we talked about how Syntax developed a functional information system that provides investors with a way to identify and diversify related business risks in order to improve return over a full market cycle by better diversifying equity market exposures. Syntax is one important innovation. There are others. Gaining exposure to markets in ways that may improve your return is part of the equation. Defending your wealth is equally important. Market risk is what happens in bear markets. Avoiding big mistakes that come in secular bear markets is a must on your long-term path to financial success. Now let's talk about ways to grow and defend your wealth.

To protect against market risk, one must be adaptive in their approach, overriding what many of us have been brainwashed to believe: that you have to buy and hold. As we discussed, markets cycle above and below a predictable long-term growth trend. It is investor emotion that drives prices to become extremely overvalued, and it is investor panic that sends prices back to and below the long-term growth trend. A buy-and-hold approach works best when your entry point is at or below the market's long-term growth trend. It is when prices and valuations get bid up above trend that investors should adjust the game plan and focus on defending their wealth, especially when their time horizon is short. Cycles are inevitable. Where we sit in the cycle matters, but those cycles can be managed.

> A buy-and-hold approach works best when your entry point is at or below the market's long-term growth trend. It is when prices and valuations get bid up above trend that investors should adjust the game plan and focus on defending their wealth, especially when their time horizon is short.

It is easy to identify where we may sit in the market cycle, but it is nearly impossible to know when the cycle will end. However, we can measure when the odds for higher returns are in our favor and when they are not. You can use available tools and strategies to help you position your portfolio defensively when the market cycle is extended and position aggressively when valuations and forward return opportunities are attractive. This will present when the market cycle is at or below its long-term growth trend.

Remember, overcoming a 50 percent loss requires a 100 percent return. With inflation factored in, that can take many years—years a preretiree or retiree may not have. Thanks to the merciless math of loss, we know that, ultimately, it is far more important to minimize losses than to capture the best gains. But no one said the path would be easy.

Psychological processes like those we've already discussed continue to dictate investor behavior, causing them to herd in and out of investments. As James Montier explains in *The Little Book of Behavioral Investing*, "We tend to hang onto our views too long simply because we spend time and effort coming up with those views in the first place. This leads to confirmation bias and an anchoring to strongly held beliefs even if the evidence fails to support them anymore."[48] The extreme selling that took place in 2008 and early 2009, or during the tech-buying frenzy of 1999, are emblematic of this truth. These incidents also point to another issue we discussed briefly in the previous chapter: following the herd. Let's take a quick look at the impact of that tendency.

## All the Cool Kids Are Doing It

*It is remarkable how much long-term advantage people like us have gotten by trying to be consistently not stupid, instead of trying to be very intelligent.*
**—Charlie Munger**

When it comes to investing, peer pressure takes its toll. Of course, peer pressure can be beneficial. Social cues help us fit in and feel comfortable. They can even fuel our success. As such, when we see a group of people behaving in the same way, we assume that there's sound rationale behind their decision-making. So we follow along.

Remember the TV show *Candid Camera*? One famous episode

---

48    Montier, 2010.

showed how silly humans can be when it comes to emulating each other's actions. In one skit, three actors follow an unsuspecting man into an elevator, but instead of turning around and facing the sliding door once inside—typical elevator protocol—the three actors stand facing the back wall of the elevator. Befuddled, the unsuspecting man slowly and casually turns around and faces the back wall of the elevator too.

The *Candid Camera* crew pulls the same prank again with another guy, and he too dutifully turns around and faces the back wall of the elevator as if commanded to do so by the others.

The skit shows that people have a tendency to follow completely irrational and illogical behavior just because they see other people doing it. None of us is immune to the power of peer pressure— probably because most of the time it *is* perfectly logical and beneficial for us to follow the crowd.

If you're wading in the ocean and you see everyone around you suddenly turn and start running for dry land, it's probably a good idea to follow them. If you're at a baseball game and everyone in your section ducks for cover, you should probably duck too. Most of the time, groups of people have good reason for having the same behaviors. Most of the time. But when it comes to investing, charging along with the herd can be downright dangerous.

Since the beginning of civilization, man has tried to understand and predict how others might behave in certain situations. That's what business is all about—anticipating the behaviors of others. Investing too. Markets are made up of people; thus, human tendencies are reflected in the pricing and volatility of securities.

Investors would like to believe that they and others act rationally, even in the most stressful situations. But throughout this book, we've seen how irrational investors become when they get caught up in speculative markets. The ridiculous amounts of leverage that eventually collapsed Long Term Capital Management in 1998, the great tech bubble in 2000, and the housing market bubble and Great Financial Crisis that followed in 2008. These are just a few examples of human behavioral tendencies and herd mentality.

Chasing into the market at periods of extreme overvaluation usually doesn't turn out very well. The exact opposite is true at market bottoms. Some of the greatest investment opportunities present when the majority of investors sell, despite compelling valuations.

When you avoid buying into the hype—and by the same token, the paranoia—you can prevent significant losses and take advantage of the greatest investment opportunities that present when the majority of investors panic. This is trying to be consistently not stupid. This is where you can find an edge.

Every once in a while, typically every ten years or so, an up cycle goes on for an extended period of time and to great extreme. People believe "This time is different." But inevitably, it is not different. In markets, most excesses are to the upside. Understanding that markets move to extremes and then return back to their long-term growth trend is core to helping you avoid harm. And knowing corrections rarely stop at the long-term growth trend line can help you profit from them.

When the cool kids are saying, "It's different this time," like they did in 2000 and again in 2008, channel your inner Charlie Munger and know that it isn't. The goal is to be "consistently not stupid." Understanding where we sit within

> When the cool kids are saying, "It's different this time," like they did in 2000 and again in 2008, channel your inner Charlie Munger and know that it isn't.

the market cycle can help. Putting an adaptive investment game plan in place will help you navigate market cycles. It's easy to do if you don't let your emotions get in the way.

Now that we've looked at market cycles, what valuations tells us about forward returns, and a better way to gain core equity market exposure, we can turn our attention to how trend-following strategies may help you better manage your downside risk of loss. By combining various investments together in your portfolio, you have the ability to shape a return stream that is suitable for the amount of risk you are willing to take. This is where investment strategy planning, income needs, time frame, and the goals most important to you come into play.

I encourage you to consider an adaptive investment approach that enables you to seek a suitable level of growth while maintaining a level of protection against downside risk. Do it in a disciplined way that limits exposure to overpriced assets, and then increases exposure when assets are attractively priced. Trend following is one way to help you risk manage your exposures in both bull and bear market cycles. Let's talk about how it works.

## Trend Following

Market trends persist over time and stem from changes in risk premiums or the amount of return investors demand as compensation for the risk they take on. Risk premiums vary a great deal over time in response to new market information, changes in the economic environment, or even changes in investor sentiment. When risk premiums increase or decrease, stocks and bonds and other assets have to be priced again. Investors react to the changes gradually, and this creates trends.

Rules-based trend-following strategies don't predict what will happen. Rather, they react to what prices are telling us about supply and demand—whether there are more buyers than sellers or vice versa. In general, they seek upside potential via an investment process that offers downside protection. Academics call it "time-series momentum," but the investment approach is most commonly known as "trend following." Trend-following trading seeks to capture the majority of a market trend—up or down—for profit. Such strategies work in all major asset classes—stocks, bonds, currency, and commodities. And trend following is one of just a few investment factors that work consistently over time.

In a January 2016 study titled "The Enduring Effect of Time-Series Momentum on Stock Returns Over Nearly One Hundred Years," researchers reviewed the effectiveness of trend following from 1927 to 2014, analyzing sixty-seven markets across four major asset classes: various commodities, equity indexes, bond markets, and currency combinations. They found that it worked in all markets—large and small, anywhere and everywhere.[49] Time-series stock-momentum strategies produced significant profits in the US markets from 1927 to 2014, exceeding returns from other factors such as value and size. They also found that the strategy was profitable regardless of formation and holding periods for sixteen different combinations.

The researchers' work demonstrates the benefits of focusing on investment processes, not emotions. With the right processes in place, paying attention to a number of indicators that dictate your next move, you can build a simple portfolio that will carry you through life. Ultimately, none of those indicators is perfect—nothing is. But

---

49    Ian D'Souza, Voraphat Srichanachaichok, George Wang, and Yaqiong (Chelsea) Yao, "The Enduring Effect of Time-Series Momentum on Stock Returns Over Nearly 100-Years," Asian Finance Association (AsianFA) 2016 Conference, January 26, 2016, http://dx.doi.org/10.2139/ssrn.2720600.

together they're very good. And if you can harness several trading strategies, you can make better diversification a part of your plan. Every week, I list my favorite stock, investor sentiment, bond and gold market indicators—or trade signals—in my *Trade Signals* blog post. Let's take a look at a few of them now.

## S&P 500 Index Composite 50-Day vs. Simple Two-Hundred-Day Moving Average Cross ("The Golden Cross")

The Golden Cross is significant. Why? Over a long period of time (since 1929), all the gains for this market have come when the fifty-day moving average line was above the two-hundred-day moving average line. The Golden Cross process is easy to follow and implement. Buy signals occur when the intermediate-term fifty-day moving-average-price trend line crosses above the long-term two-hundred-day moving-average-price trend line. Sell signals occur when the fifty-day moving average line crosses below the two-hundred-day moving average line. Many investors use it as a way to risk-manage their investment exposures. The approach seeks to provide exposure to US large-cap equities while simultaneously avoiding significant and prolonged drawdowns by tactically allocating to short- or intermediate-term US Treasuries.

The following chart captures the S&P 500 Index fifty-day versus two-hundred-day moving average from 1929 and 1999 to the present. The dotted line in the bottom half of the chart represents the two-hundred-day moving average line, and the solid line in the bottom half of the chart is the fifty-day moving average line.

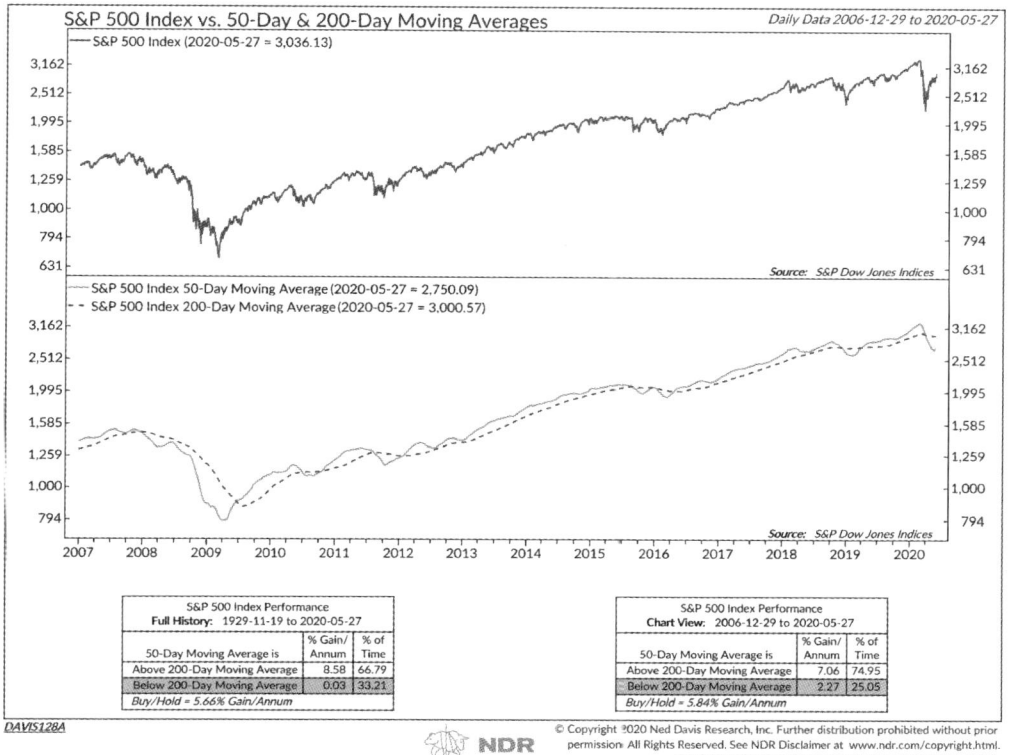

S&P 500 Index vs. 50-Day & 200-Day Moving Averages — Daily Data 2006-12-29 to 2020-05-27

S&P 500 Index (2020-05-27 = 3,036.13)

Source: S&P Dow Jones Indices

S&P 500 Index 50-Day Moving Average (2020-05-27 = 2,750.09)
S&P 500 Index 200-Day Moving Average (2020-05-27 = 3,000.57)

Source: S&P Dow Jones Indices

| S&P 500 Index Performance Full History: 1929-11-19 to 2020-05-27 | % Gain/ Annum | % of Time |
|---|---|---|
| 50-Day Moving Average is | | |
| Above 200-Day Moving Average | 8.58 | 66.79 |
| Below 200-Day Moving Average | 0.03 | 33.21 |
| Buy/Hold = 5.66% Gain/Annum | | |

| S&P 500 Index Performance Chart View: 2006-12-29 to 2020-05-27 | % Gain/ Annum | % of Time |
|---|---|---|
| 50-Day Moving Average is | | |
| Above 200-Day Moving Average | 7.06 | 74.95 |
| Below 200-Day Moving Average | 2.27 | 25.05 |
| Buy/Hold = 5.84% Gain/Annum | | |

DAVIS128A

NDR

© Copyright 2020 Ned Davis Research, Inc. Further distribution prohibited without prior permission. All Rights Reserved. See NDR Disclaimer at www.ndr.com/copyright.html. For data vendor disclaimers refer to www.ndr.com/vendorinfo/

Now look at the box below the chart on the right-hand side, which shows S&P 500 Index performance from December 29, 2006, to May 27, 2020. You can see that when the fifty-day line is above the longer-term, two-hundred-day trend line, the S&P 500 Index has annualized gains of 7.06 percent, and the market was in an uptrend 74.95 percent of the time.

Meanwhile, all the losses have occurred when that fifty-day line drops below the two-hundred-day line, creating a "sell" signal. It's a simple rule that anyone can follow to manage core market exposure. And it enables you to stay invested when the predominant trend is up.

It's important to note that this process is not perfect (nor is any investment process), and there will be a number of false trades. Risk-management processes such as this are particularly useful when the equity market cycle is overvalued and prices have moved far above normal long-term trend growth. The real benefits come in avoiding the major market down cycles, and that is what this process can help you do. Let's look at another popular trend-following process.

## S&P 500 Index Composite vs. Simple Two-Hundred-Day Moving Average

*My metric for everything I look at is the two-hundred-day moving average of closing prices. I've seen too many things go to zero, stocks and commodities ... If you use the two-hundred-day moving average rule, then you get out. You play defense, and you get out.*

**—Paul Tudor Jones**

Another popular trend-following process is the simple two-hundred-day moving average rule. Earlier we talked about the two-hundred-day moving average rule Paul Tudor Jones taught his students. Next is another version of the two-hundred-day rule. I favor it because it reduces the number of whipsaws that occur with the cross rule yet keeps you invested when the trend in price is bullish. In the following chart, the dashed black line depicts the two-hundred-day moving average, and the solid line represents the S&P 500 Index. A "buy" signal is created when the two-hundred-day moving-average-price line rises from a low point by 0.05 percent or more, and a "sell" signal forms when it falls from a high point by 0.05 percent or more. Focus on the upper right-hand corner of the chart and on the data boxes below. The shaded portion in the data box shows the current signal. And as you can see, the majority of returns since 1929 and all the returns since 1999 have come when the trend line has set off a "buy" signal. That two-hundred-day moving average rule can be used on individual stocks, index funds, and ETFs.

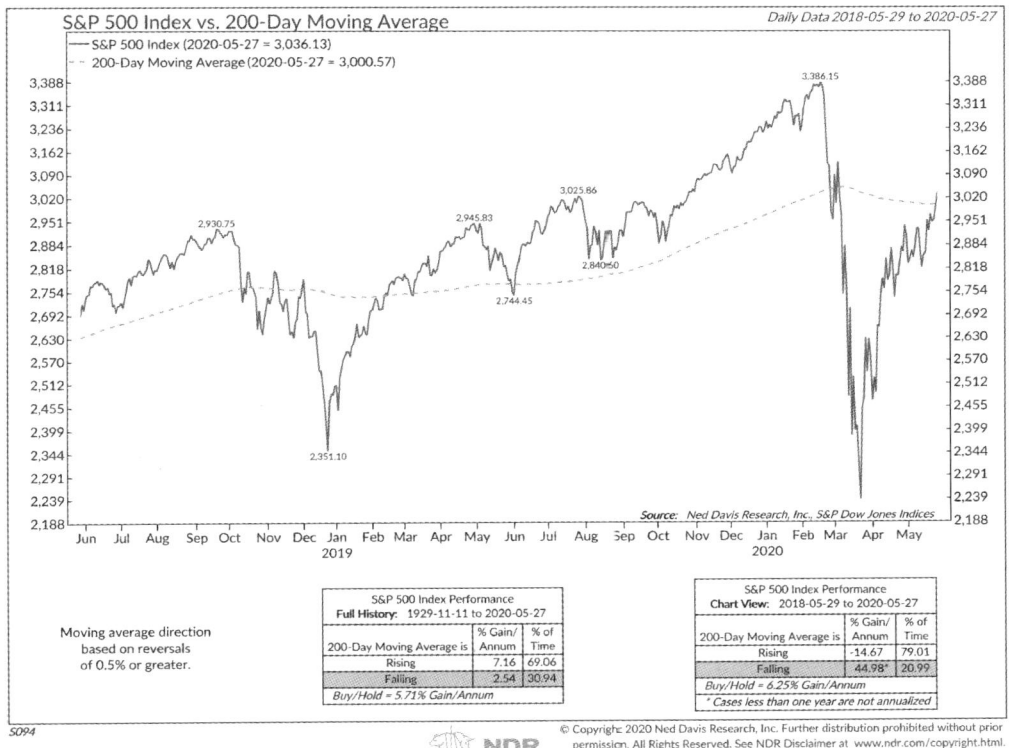

## NASDAQ Composite vs. Simple Two-Hundred-Day Moving Average

Here we look at the rule applied to the NASDAQ Composite Index. In the following chart, the dashed line depicts the two-hundred-day moving average, and the solid line represents the NASDAQ Composite. A "buy" signal is created when the two-hundred-day moving average rises from a low point by 0.05 percent or more, and a "sell" signal forms when it falls from a high point by 0.05 percent or more. Focus on the upper right-hand corner of the chart, and on the data boxes below. The shaded portion in the data box shows the current signal and data history.

NASDAQ Composite vs. 200-Day Moving Average — Daily Data 2018-05-29 to 2020-05-27

## Zweig Bond Model

Let's check out a way the trend can help identify how to position in the bond market. You may know that I'm a big fan of Ned Davis. His excellent book, *Being Right or Making Money*, is grounded in the assertion that it's not possible for investors to predict the future, but with the right strategy, it's not necessary either.[50] It's all about understanding how price can help you stay on the right side of a trend, but to do that, you have to lose your ego, build a process, and follow it. Ned Davis Research, the independent research shop he founded in 1980, is based on this concept.

---

50   Ned Davis, *Being Right or Making Money* (Hoboken: Wiley, 2014).

Ned worked with the late Marty Zweig, a legend in the investment space, on a bond model based on trend following. The Zweig Bond model is one of my favorite processes to identify when to shorten high-quality bond maturities and when to lengthen them.

Take a look at the following chart. The process is explained in the upper left-hand section of the chart "Model Indicators." The bottom section details the drawdown history and a few other statistics. For example, if you had a $100,000 investment and it declined 10 percent to $90,000 before moving higher, your drawdown would be 10 percent. Marty and Ned looked at the Barclay's Aggregate Bond Index to create the model, and you can compare the Barclay's Aggregate Bond Index Total Return's maximum drawdown to theirs. Barclays Aggregate Bond Total Return has a maximum drawdown of -14.12 percent versus the Zweig Bond Model's maximum drawdown of -5.06 percent. What you'd hope for is a higher return and a lower drawdown. The bottom left-hand corner also lists the hypothetical growth of $1,000. The GPA percent shows the hypothetical comparison of the Zweig Bond Model to the Barclays Aggregate Total Return Index. The model outperformed buying and holding the index by a wide margin. The arrow highlights the data. The shaded box shows the active signal.

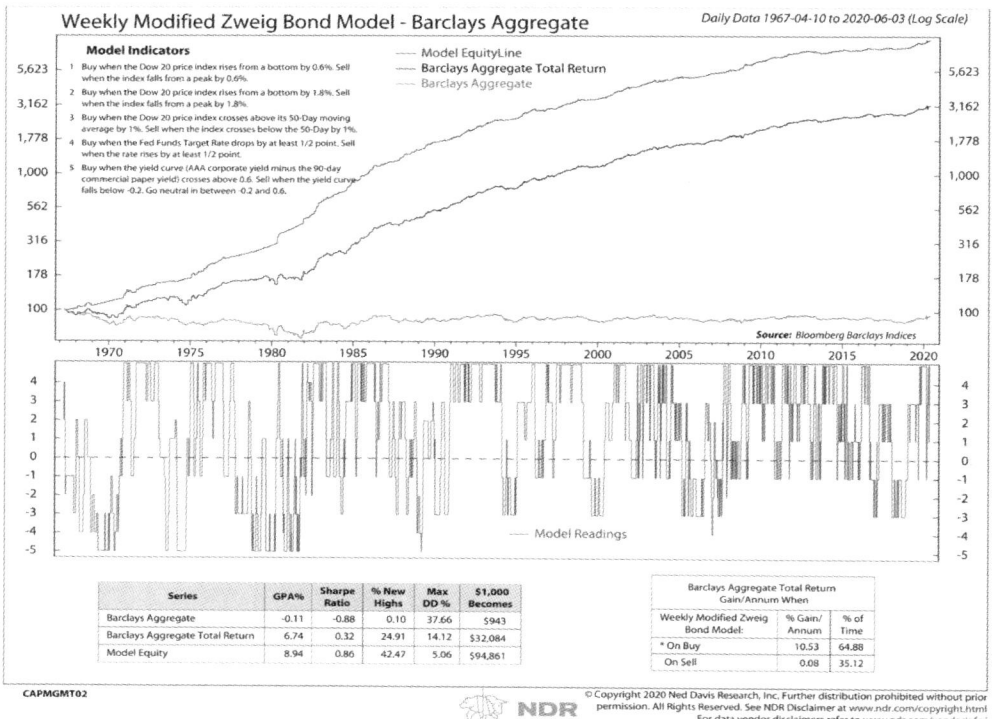

Here's a quick story that illustrates just how useful this model can be: At the end of 2014, twenty-five out of twenty-five Wall Street fixed-income analysts said that interest rates were going to go from 2.75 percent up to an average of 3.25 percent. All of them were wrong. Interest rates actually dropped from 2.75 percent down to 2.25 percent. But my Zweig Bond Model was right. It doesn't have an opinion; it simply follows the rules—which you can see in the upper left-hand corner of the chart. The box labeled "Barclays Aggregate Total Return" tells you if the model is on a buy or a sell signal. The model has been bullish on long bonds most of 2019 and is bullish at the time of this writing. Meanwhile, many people have a fundamental view that interest rates are going to move higher. Others believe rates will move even lower. With yields on the ten-year Treasury under 2 percent, what do you do with the bond portion of your portfolio allocation? Trend following can help.

I favor a rules-based, disciplined process that turns to price to determine what's happening and prescribe a course of action. My go-to bond indicator is the Zweig Bond Model. You can find more how-to information on the CMG Wealth web site at https://www. cmgwealth.com/ri-category/trade-signals/. Let's explore one last easy-to-follow strategy.

Though no one trend-following strategy is perfect, trend following can help you navigate market cycles and avoid the really big mistakes. I like to diversify to several different trend-following processes, including using moving average trend-following rules to trade the gold market, which I share in my *Trade Signals* blog each week. With some go-to trade signals to dictate your decisions (and a

> Though no one trend-following strategy is perfect, trend following can help you navigate market cycles and avoid the really big mistakes.

clear understanding of where we sit in the equity market cycle) rather than your emotions or the herd at large, you'll be better equipped to manage your risk and make smart investment decisions. This is especially important if you are a preretiree or retiree.

But we're not quite done with the *what to do about it* question posed in Chapter 7. It's time to pull everything we've discussed together and talk about building and managing a diversified total portfolio. In the next chapter, I share my broader thinking about wealth, and we'll discuss how to mix things together, size them, and apply trend following and other strategies designed to achieve a desired return relative to the level of risk that is acceptable to you.

# CHAPTER 10

# What Matters Most

*"Investing is the intersection of economics and psychology.*
*"The economics, the valuation of the business, is not hard. The psychology—How much do you buy? Do you buy it at this price? Do you wait for a lower price? What do you do when it looks like the world might end? Those are the harder things."*
**—Seth Klarman**

Throughout this book, we've talked about what does and doesn't matter in the investment landscape—from tuning out the noise to understanding how economic and market cycles work and the critical signals and processes that may help you grow and defend your wealth. We've discussed how to know when the odds are more or less in your favor so you're aware of when probable returns are high and risk is low—and vice versa. But you may still be wondering about how to pull it all together and create a portfolio that is custom-tailored to your individual goals, needs, risk tolerance, and investment time horizon. That's what we'll do here.

In this final chapter, we'll talk about a comprehensive approach to building resilient investment portfolios that target the level of return you want relative to the level of risk suitable for you.

I want to begin this chapter's discussion with a simple concept: how to think about wealth. My partners, John Mauldin, renowned financial expert and a multiple *New York Times* bestselling author; Kevin Malone, founder of Greenrock Research; and I coauthored a research paper about how to think about wealth. Here, we'll cover some key points on this crucial topic.

Over the years, we've learned that no two people are alike, financially or otherwise, and we have thoroughly considered that reality as we've developed investment solutions for different types of investors (available on the CMG Mauldin Portfolios Platform). When it comes to money management, there's no one-size-fits-all strategy. Investment solutions should be personal—tailored to fit your goals and needs. But to determine what that looks like, let's keep Seth Klarman's quotes in mind and cover some general information to set the stage.

## Setting the Stage

The vast majority of wealth—75 percent—is concentrated in the hands of preretirees and retirees. I'm one of them, as are many of my firms' private clients. As you can imagine, their financial needs differ from investors in the accumulation phase of their lives.

While individual circumstances dictate strategy, everyone—regardless of age or financial circumstances—should think about the money they've allocated toward savings as separate and apart from the rest of their investment portfolio. Savings needs—like next year's college tuition, funds for a new house, or a rainy day fund—may dictate that investors keep more or less capital liquid and readily available. Now, let's focus in on the investment portion of your wealth. We've got a few more basics to cover before we get into some portfolio ideas.

## Defend Your Wealth

It's hard to make money and even more difficult to keep it. Protecting capital from inflation and taxation poses a great enough challenge; you must avoid compounding it with factors such as imprudence while choosing investments.

The real risk of investing is losing your capital permanently, without recourse to ever recover it. That's why it's crucial to understand the magic of compound interest and just how merciless the math becomes when you lose. As discussed in Chapter 4, defend your capital against significant losses to allow compound interest to work in your favor over time.

> Defend your capital against significant losses to allow compound interest to work in your favor over time.

How do you do that? View your investments as a collection of assets, each with its own purpose. When you do, those diverse components combine to create a portfolio that is better equipped to withstand inevitable market turbulence and the pressures exerted upon them over time. But doing so effectively requires the right information and support.

When you are younger and new to investing, you want to

believe the Wall Street analysts, rating agencies, government statistics, etc. But as you get older, you're bound to realize that many of them are less than truthful; therefore, you must approach all information carefully and with skepticism. Investing requires a steady hand. When you choose an investment advisor, you're not giving them capital to play with, you are entrusting them with a lifetime's worth of savings—that must be defended. Make sure your advisor is focused on protecting what you have spent years accumulating.

We've already discussed the reality that equities will produce a relatively consistent return over time—approximately 10.1 percent since 1926.[51] However, those returns, as you'll see below, are not consistent because, as you know, investor behavior causes equity market prices to rise above the natural return rate, and such escalations eventually give way to correction. And corrections don't generally drop back to the natural return rate. Thanks to human behavior, they tend to descend below it. The best investment return opportunities come when prices correct below the natural rate of return, and the worst returns come when prices are above that diagonal line. Where we sit in the long-term investment cycle at any given time matters, and you can use the data to your advantage. What do you do when it looks like the world might end? That's when you want to aggressively overweight to equities.

As you've seen throughout this book, we can determine where we are relative to that long-term growth trend line, and a prudent wealth manager takes this into consideration as they set your investment plan. There are times to overweight equities—to play more offense than defense—and times to underweight equity exposure (to play more defense than offense). Thus, I believe investors should be

---

51   Cumulative Investment Returns Since 1926, Ned Davis Research, Bloomberg
     Finance LP, Bureau of Labor Statistics, S&P DJ Indices.

adaptive in their investment approach. As my dear friend and partner John Mauldin likes to say, "There are times in the investment cycle when friends should not let friends buy and hold." And there are other times they should do just that.

> There are times in the investment cycle when friends should not let friends buy and hold.

In sports, defense wins championships. The same is true in investing. And the greatest teams enter each game and season with a well thought out game plan. I believe you should do the same with your investment game plan. Let's take a closer look at an approach to consider.

## The 80 Core–20 Explore Concept

### HOW WE THINK ABOUT WEALTH

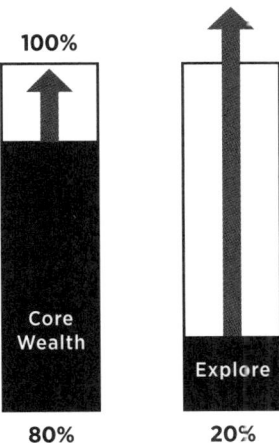

Not a specific recommendation for you to buy or sell any security. For discussion purposes only.

At CMG, our investment mindset is simple—we call it "Core and Explore." Objective number one is to defend your core wealth. Let's say that represents around 80 percent of your investable assets. The goal is to seek growth and protect the downside in such a way that your 80 percent core grows back to 100 percent, ideally in four to six years (though, of course, there's never a guarantee). With your core wealth defended, you are afforded the ability to "explore" with the remaining 20 percent of your wealth. The previous graphic paints the picture.

You may be younger or older—more aggressive or more conservative. Your game plan may be 70–30 percent or 60–40 percent or 50–50. Or you may be even more conservative and allocate 90–10 or 100–0. Everyone's needs and interests are different. You have the ability to dial up or dial down the reward-to-risk ratio at any time, but the concept remains the same.

Meanwhile, the "explore" portion of your portfolio is the fun stuff. Here, you can consider transformational investment ideas in technology, biotech, healthcare, etc. *Exploring* doesn't mean you're taking a gamble; this is about thoughtfully positioning in strategically sourced and intelligently researched investment opportunities.

What could those opportunities entail? A direct investment in a pioneering bioagriculture company, a world-changing product, service, or project—a medication with the potential to save lives; a real estate opportunity or a piece of technology that could transform communication, data storage, or secure trade. They tend to be disrupters that improve our way of living. And they're the kinds of investments that may create great wealth. Investing in the broad equity market indices isn't going to do that for you.

The reason I favor Core and Explore is that it's a plan that can keep you on track, even when markets are dislocating. Recall the early days of companies like Netflix or Apple or Amazon. Who had the courage to invest in Amazon at its IPO in 1997? Or to follow the lead of smart investors who invested in the early private equity rounds? If your core is defended, it enables the ability to seek explore opportunities knowing full well not all of them will win.

Amazon is one of the great investment stories out there today, but it was far from a sure thing. When it went public in 1997, it was at a split-adjusted price of $1.50. As of this writing (Q2 of 2020), it is above $2,500 per share. An exceptional example of the potential of exploring. It's important to note few investments will be like Amazon. Over the last ten years Amazon compounded at 31 percent. This likely will not happen often.

The path to that great success wasn't smooth sailing. Amazon reached $86 per share in 1999, and then declined to less than $6 per share after the tech bubble burst in 2001. There are many reasons to sell, and seeing your stock drop from $86 to $6 is a big one. The real question is, could you have held on for the ride? Many couldn't. But what if they had been more confident in their core?

I argue that if you follow our investment mindset—if your core wealth (the 80 percent) is defended and you are confident it will grow it back to 100 percent—and you explore with the remaining 20 percent, you put yourself in a better emotional position to weather the storm. You allow yourself the patience that may be required for your explore opportunities to grow.

Assume you were worth $2 million in 1997 and you allocated 3 percent of your wealth to Amazon. That $60,000 investment would be worth $100 million today. And if Amazon went to zero, your portfolio would be down just 3 percent that year. With your core wealth defended, you remain in the game even if things go south. And if one or more of your explore investments succeeds, it may be a game changer for you and your family. Not all investments win, of course, so make sure you diversify and consider adding to the explore investments that are advancing their business models. And above all, stick to the game plan you put in place for yourself.

At CMG, we only consider explore investment opportunities we believe have the potential to produce returns of ten times or greater over the coming ten years. I encourage you to think similarly when considering your options. Of course, there are no guarantees. That's why it is important to size your allocations carefully. In addition, it's important to develop a handful of trusted relationships that will aid you in sourcing, researching, and doing the deep due diligence needed to minimize mistakes and maximize potential. To learn more about our network, send me a note at Blumenthal@cmgwealth.com and mention this book.

Now that we've broadly covered the concept of explore investment opportunities, let's conclude with a few ideas on how you can build the core portion of your portfolio. As we do, keep the wisdom from Seth Klarman top of mind. Investing is emotional. Following are just a few ideas for you to think about as you begin building.

## Building Your Core

Over the years, the world has advanced in ways that make more strategies accessible to more people, broadening opportunities for things like index funds; ETFs; trend following risk-managed trading strategies; and global all-asset managers, who look at various investment opportunities around the world—such as bonds or stocks of different countries, gold, and currencies. That's a real benefit, giving investors more tools for diversification and at lower costs. And it's especially important given how low interest rates are today. Bonds used to be a great diversifier. But there is simply no way today's ultra-low-yielding bonds can provide the same value to your portfolio that the same bonds yielding 6 percent did just ten years ago. Thus, there is the need to source higher returns with a similar risk profile to the one bonds provided in years past.

So how do you allocate core portfolio funds among: equities, fixed income, and trading strategies? It comes down to the asset classes and strategies you combine to build your core portfolio. And as you consider weightings and percentages within your different portfolio positions, it's important to factor into your thinking where we sit in terms of valuations and long-term trend growth. Let's think back to Chapter 6 and what current valuations tell us about forward returns. As we've discussed, stocks cycle over time above and below their natural long-term growth trend, moving from periods of undervalued to overvalued and then undervalued again. Factor this into your thinking and increase your exposure to equities when valuations are low, risk is low, and forward returns are high. Reduce your exposure to equities when valuations are high, risk is high and forward return probabilities are low. And consider utilizing trend following strategies to help you mitigate risk.

As of this writing, valuations are at the second-most expensive rate in history. And they could go higher. However, probable five- and ten-year coming stock market returns are in the 0 to 3 percent range before inflation is factored in. That doesn't mean the market won't go up 20 percent in the next six months. It just means that over the next five to ten years, returns are likely to be in the low and the ride to those low returns will probably be bumpy.

In the following pages, you will find a description of several core investment strategies we at CMG consider when building your core portfolio. We've already looked at how Syntax's better diversification process may enhance index returns above the long-term 10.1 percent annualized return line. We'll consider several additional portfolio ideas and how you might combine different asset classes and managed strategies to achieve a certain return relative to risk objective. Let's look at the math.

Textbooks teach us about the efficient frontier. This concept is best reflected in the following chart, which illustrates the impact of diversifying investments. You can see how return (the vertical axis) increases as we move from a 100 percent allocation to bonds up to 100 percent allocation to stocks, as does risk (the horizontal axis). Think of the convex dotted line as the efficient frontier for various combinations of stocks and bonds, ranging from 100 percent bonds to 100 percent stocks. The gap between the convex dotted line and the diagonal dotted line represents the benefit of diversification.

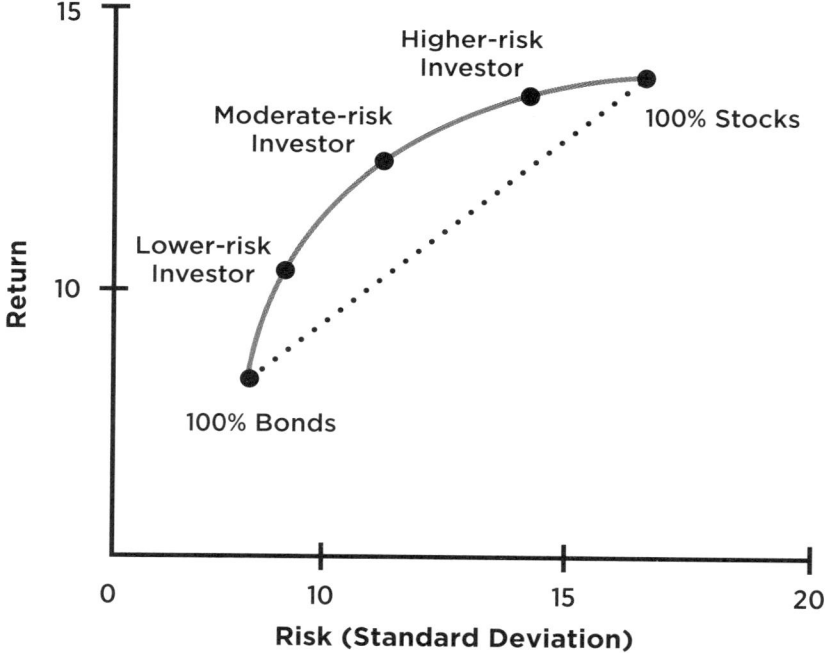

To recap, the convex line is better, because for any point on the diagonal line, you can find a point on the convex line that has either a higher return, a lower risk, or some combination of the two. The idea here is that by combining different assets, you can structure a portfolio to meet your return and risk objectives by changing the size and weightings to various risk assets and strategies. You have the ability to dial up and dial down return and risk. It depends on your investment objectives and time frame, but this is what we are after when we talk about more predictably growing and defending your core wealth.

To hit that "moderate-risk investor" target in the past chart, one simply needed to invest 50 percent in stocks and 50 percent in bonds. However, with the ten-year Treasury bond yielding less than 1 percent, there is simply no way bonds can help a portfolio the way they have in years past. The Federal Reserve has distorted the ability of traditional bond investing to be efficient.

In the previous chart, you'll see three dots, noting "Lower-risk," "Moderate-risk," and "Higher-risk" along the efficient frontier line. That's what we are after when we think about building a core portfolio. There are ways to dial up or dial down your return/risk ratio depending on how you size an allocation and which strategies you use to build your core. Let's consider a few asset classes and strategies.

## High and Growing Dividend-Paying Stocks

My partner Kevin Malone from Greenrock Research has been managing portfolios of high and growing dividend-paying stocks for twenty years. These are companies that have a history of paying high dividends to their shareholders and increasing the dividend payouts (thus the name high and growing dividend payers). In an excellent research paper titled "Risk Will Be Redefined and the Definition of Volatility as the Measure of Risk Will Be Incomplete," Kevin noted that the efficient frontier gave us what we thought was a useful tool to help clients understand the risk they were taking with their investment portfolio, and it gave financial planners comfort, ensuring them that they had predictability in helping clients achieve their investment goals. Stock markets and bond markets had volatility, but it was the volatility of stock market declines that worried clients and planners alike.

But after a thirty-five-year bull market in bonds and yields near 0 percent, the risk of loss in the bond market should rates rise has never been greater. The assumption of the efficient frontier—that returns would be normalized—created the problem we see with this tool today. The reality is that returns are not normal and big losses occur much more frequently than we thought. To solve for this, we can think differently about how we allocate to achieve an efficient outcome.

The following data shows the returns of the S&P 500 index for the last six full decades—the 1960s to 2010s—and an assumption of return for the current decade, the 2020s. The assumption we are using for the 2020s comes from Research Affiliates. The annualized return for the sixty years of actual returns, 1960–2019, is 9.85 percent, very close to the most common return assumption used in investment planning, 10 percent. The problem is when you review the individual returns from each decade, no decade achieves the 10 percent return factored into most financial planning models.

## S&P 500 10-YEAR & 20-YEAR TOTAL RETURNS

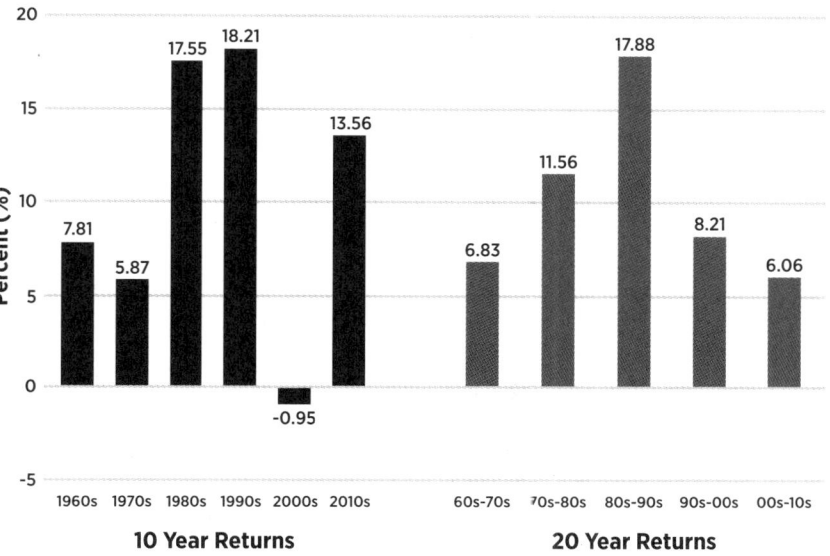

How do we get more consistency in equity returns?

This above chart shows us the lack of consistency we discussed in a paper titled "Equity Returns Have Been Misunderstood." There are two factors to total return in equities: dividends and appreciation. Dividends have more predictability than appreciation, and therefore a portfolio focused on current dividend yield and prospective dividend growth in theory would experience more consistent returns. We have been managing a global portfolio using this investment thesis for twenty years, so we can look at that data. In addition, Jeremy Siegel, a professor at the Wharton School of the University of Pennsylvania, did a study that is a variation on our theme using the entire history of the S&P 500. The next chart shows the decade returns in ten- and twenty-year periods.

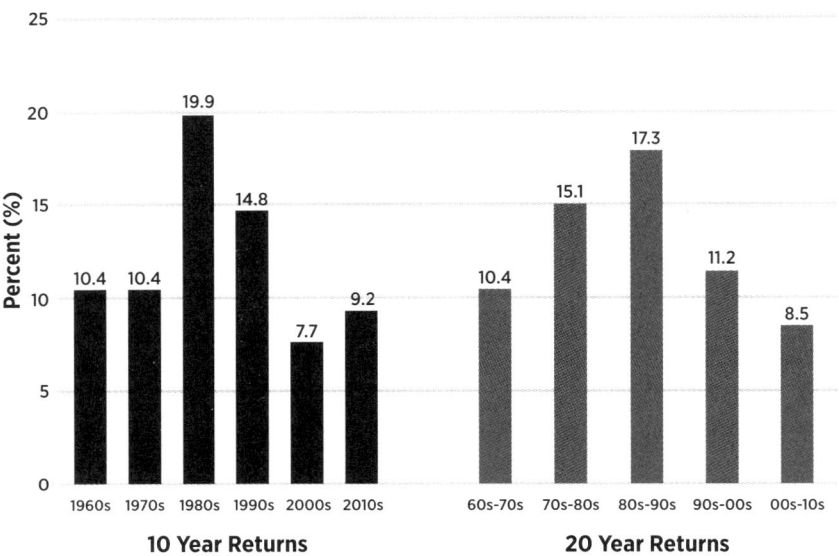

**DIVIDEND PORTFOLIO**
**10-YEAR & 20-YEAR TOTAL RETURNS**

**10 Year Returns**          **20 Year Returns**

As you see, the returns in decades and in twenty-year periods are more consistent than the returns of the index. The only twenty-year period when the dividend strategy did not achieve the 10 percent goal was the last twenty years, when it achieved a return of 8.42 percent. In four of the six ten-year periods, the dividend strategy achieved the desired 10 percent return, and in the 2010s the return was 9.2 percent—very close. It is worth noting that Dr. Siegel's work shows returns of 3.9 percent and 12.6 percent for the decades of the 2000s and 2010s, while we had returns of 7.7 percent and 9.2 percent. For the twenty-year period, Dr. Siegel's work showed a return of 8.1 percent while our return was 8.5 percent. So, Dr. Siegel's methodology showed a similar yet slightly lower total return while our portfolios showed a more consistent return.

What should our measure of risk be?

It is important to say that if you wanted to use the long-term return of 10 percent, using the dividend method would be reasonable. That said, the best measure of future return is one that provides consistency, one you and (if you are an advisor) your clients can measure over rolling three- and five-year time frames to determine if you are reaching your goal.

That method is a combination of dividend yield and dividend growth. If we know the current dividend yield of a portfolio and make a reasonable assumption of prospective dividend growth, we can show future dividend yields from portfolios. The next chart shows that data using our current high and growing dividend portfolio yield projected over the decade of the 2020s.

## GREENROCK HIGH & GROWING DIVIDEND
## DIVIDEND INCREASE 0.25% PER YEAR

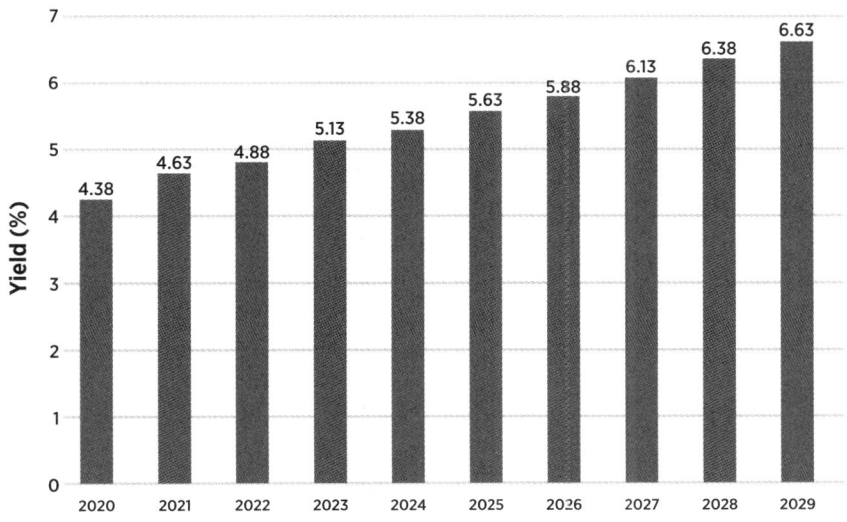

As you see, the current dividend yield is 4.38 percent. If we grow dividends at 0.25 percent per year, the chart shows the dividend yields annually over the decade of the 2020s. This portfolio is expected to have a compounded annualized return in the form of dividends of 5.75 percent per year over the decade. This represents the return with the assumption of no appreciation or depreciation, and the final dividend yield will be 6.63 percent. Now it is true that this portfolio could produce losses, if stock prices decline. In addition, our assumption is that the portfolio will increase by 25 basis points (bps) per year, but we have no expectation that each stock will have that level of dividend increase. In addition, dividends could grow at lower levels than 25 bps per year. Our assumption of 25 bps dividend growth per year is lower than historical dividend growth of 8-10 percent. We are using this lower number because we believe GDP growth and earnings growth will be lower in the future, and therefore dividend growth will be lower as well.

If you are an advisor, how do you communicate this with clients?

The data above show two things. First, growing dividend strategies achieve higher long-term returns but underperform the S&P 500 at times—and some of those times are as long as a decade. Your clients will need to be prepared and comfortable with this reality. As a note of perspective, there is no active strategy that always outperforms an index, so this reality also will be worth mentioning to clients. The second thing to discuss with clients is that annually we can show dividend growth. Our assumption above of 25 bps per year is a target, and we can produce a report annually to show whether we've reached that level. It is the consistency of dividend growth that has allowed us to achieve much higher consistency of return over the last two decades, and this is what you will want to show clients.

When we think about traditional Efficient Frontier model return assumptions, we conclude that an assumed return of 10 percent S&P 500 index return is not a viable assumption. Greenrock's growing dividend method provides an equity investment strategy that is more predictable, which allows you to manage client expectations in a reasonable manner.

## Other Strategies for Consideration

There are a number of other investment strategies designed to seek growth and protect against downside risk of loss. One that we have been utilizing at CMG for nearly thirty years trades the intermediate-term trends in the high-yield bond market. Invest in high-yield bond funds and/or ETFs when the trend price is up. Trade to cash alternatives when the trend in price is down. High yield is an outstanding asset class, and the approach is designed to seek growth and limit downside risk of loss. This is an anchor strategy in most of our clients' portfolios. Note that the strategy itself is simple, but as Seth Klarman pointed out in this chapter's intro quote, it's executing on the trade signals that's the hard part. It requires discipline and the knowing that not every trade wins. Our process at CMG is proprietary, but a simple fifty- or one hundred-day moving average entry/exit trigger does a pretty good job, too.

Ned Davis Research's "Big Mo" indicator has served me well, especially in 2000 and 2008. "Mo" stands for momentum. It is a price-based indicator that looks at the price trend in the many sectors that make up the S&P 500 Index. Markets are healthiest when most stocks are in up trends.

My firm worked with NDR to co-create what we feel is a more functional model from a trading perspective. It individually plots the short, intermediate, and long-term price trends of twenty-four sub-industry sectors that make up the S&P 500 large cap index. The calculation agent for the index is S&P Dow Jones Indices and it is called the Ned Davis Research CMG Large Cap Long/Flat index. We use the process to risk-manage our large-cap stock market exposure.

The goal is to participate in bull market cycles and minimize risk in bear market cycles.

Another strategy we utilize in our core portfolios is a multi-manager approach that combines different trading strategies. These are active ETF investment strategists who seek growth and manage risk in different ways. With current high valuations and the coming reset of the debt and pension challenges, we believe this is an effective way to get from there to the other side of what Mauldin calls the Great Reset.

You can access equity-hedged strategies in mutual funds or ETFs. A new approach we favor gains exposure to the US total stock market (large-, mid- and small-sized companies) using Syntax's diversification approach, while hedging ongoing market downside risk with stock options.

You can also incorporate trend and momentum indicators to gain exposures to gold, fixed income, FAANG stocks, high and growing dividend ETFs, and commodities. Another strategy we like has a two-tiered investment approach that gauges macro risk to determine specific index ETFs in which to invest. The strategy can invest 100 percent in equities or 100 percent in fixed income and has the ability to move to cash in bearish environments.

In addition, there are all-asset strategies that position in the US and globally, with the goal of identifying the catalysts that drive market cycles at the asset class level. Once identified, they seek to invest in undervalued asset classes via ETFs.

When the stock market reverts back to below its long-term trend, traditional buy-and-hold investing will offer a higher return, lower risk outcome. Then, consider underweighting risk-managed and hedged equity market exposures. An experienced advisor with the right technology can help determine whether you are on the right path in terms of building a core portfolio that is appropriate for you. The idea I want to leave you with is that you have many tools available to build your efficient 'core' portfolio. Remember, the objective of your core is to defend and carefully grow your 80 percent back to 100 percent, enabling you to explore with the 20 percent. Before you build your portfolio, let's consider what your risk/return profile might look like.

# Identifying the Conservative, Moderate, and Growth Investor

We talked about how your core portfolio can be created to target a desired return for a desired level of risk. That risk level depends on the mix of assets and strategies you have. Since your core will most likely compose the largest portion of your overall portfolio, you need to think carefully about your time frame and return/risk objectives. You will need to figure out whether you should allocate 80 percent to your core—a moderate approach—or whether you are more conservative or growth-focused. Following are some guidelines to help you figure out which approach you should take.

## Conservative

This portfolio is designed for the investor seeking lower, safer returns with minimal drawdowns. The objective is to protect assets in all markets. The portfolio is expressly developed for assets that will be used for another purpose at some point in the near future. The goal of this portfolio is to provide returns that are better than money market and other short-term safe investment options. The appropriate investment time horizon for the CMG Mauldin Conservative Portfolio is one to five years.

In 2020, a reasonable return is in the 2 percent (tax free bonds) to 4 percent range, with very minimal downside risk. If you are conservative and allocate 90 percent to core and 10 percent to explore and earn an annualized return of 2.5 percent, your 90 percent will grow back to 100 percent in a little less than five years.

## Moderate

This portfolio is designed for the long-term investor who wants to be in a lower-volatility portfolio than long equities, but is still interested in achieving reasonable returns. The portfolio seeks growth while maintaining a level of protection in down markets. The appropriate investment time horizon for the CMG Mauldin Moderate Portfolio is five years or longer.

In 2020, a reasonable return may be in the 5 percent to 7 percent range, with an estimated 10 percent to 12 percent downside risk. If you are a moderate risk investor and allocate 80 percent to core and 20 percent to explore and earn an annualized return of 5 percent, your 80 percent will grow back to 100 percent in a little less than five years.

## Growth

This portfolio provides greater equity market exposure, but in areas that are deemed reasonably priced, particularly during tumultuous market climates. The portfolio seeks a higher level of return while aiming to balance the risks of upside potential gain with downside protection. For the foreseeable future, our equity exposure will be focused on high and growing dividend companies. The appropriate investment time horizon for the CMG Mauldin Growth Portfolio is seven to ten years or longer.

In 2020, a reasonable return may be in the 7 percent to 9 percent range with an estimated 12 percent to 15 percent downside risk. A healthy stock market reset will increase the return opportunity, but let's stick with 7 percent to 9 percent. If you are a growth investor and allocate 70 percent to core and 30 percent to explore and earn an annualized return of 7 percent, your 70 percent will grow back to 100 percent in a little more than five years.

If you are younger, you may decide to allocate 60 percent of your wealth to a growth-oriented core portfolio and 40 percent to explore. The idea is that—regardless of the ratio you choose—you can set up a game plan to intelligently defend your core. You can dial up or dial down your weightings to core and the level of growth you seek. Talk this through with your advisor and set in place a Core and Explore game plan that works for you.

## Summing It All Up—What Matters Most

In so many ways, sizing your risks appropriately is at the crux of it all. It's about determining what matters, drowning out what doesn't matter, and sticking to a disciplined investment game plan, and throughout this book we've discussed how to do that.

We started our journey with a Thai soccer team and their harrowing experience in the depths of a flooded cave during monsoon season and observed the necessity of adjusting a plan to address an ever-shifting set of conditions— a pertinent lesson in today's economic climate. We dug into Ray Dalio's crucial insights on

> In so many ways, sizing your risks appropriately is at the crux of it all. It's about determining what matters, drowning out what doesn't matter, and sticking to a disciplined investment game plan.

how the economic machine and debt cycles work and explored the merciless math of loss and the power of compound interest with my wife Susan over coffee. We went to school with world-renowned psychologists like Amos Tversky and Daniel Kahneman and prize-winning economists like Richard Thaler to learn about human nature and its impact on investment decisions. We talked about the impact of recessions and the opportunities that come in a crisis. We discussed the myriad advantages that understanding market cycles provides—that knowing they move to extremes, then return back to their long-term growth trend, is critical in helping you understand when risk is greatest and when opportunity is best.

We considered the price of Warren Buffett's favorite food—hamburger meat—and turned to market valuations, price, and a team of experts at the Mauldin Economics Strategic Investment Conference to understand what's happening today, what the future may hold, and when to play offense versus defense.

And we discussed what to do with all that pertinent information: the stuff that matters. We talked about how to diversify to mitigate risk and how key signals provide discipline to prevent poor decision-making. We talked about how trend following can help you seek growth and minimize your downside loss and how the Syntax and high and growing dividend payers approaches help you gain better diversification and potentially higher and more predicable return outcomes. And we talked about strategies that utilize stock options to hedge against major market dislocations. We've covered how all of this knowledge can inform your Core and Explore game plan.

I believe the coming restructuring of the debt and pension systems will ultimately lead to a period of high interest rates and even higher inflation. That isn't factored into the 0.70 percent ten-year Treasury yield we see in May 2020. And most investors are unprepared for this different type of investment regime. The great investor Stan Druckenmiller, former chairman and president of Duquesne Capital, said in a *Bloomberg* interview in December 2019. "I will go to my grave believing that the financial crisis happened because of bubbles made by easy money."[52] We have more than doubled down on the easy money policies that led to the 2008 Great Financial Crisis. In just three months in 2020, the Fed printed more money than they had in the last ten years. The risks in the system have seldom been greater.

But the ideas in this book aren't just applicable to one period of time; I've shared concepts and strategies to help get you from here to there no matter what the economic landscape looks like. I hope you find them helpful. Today, though, we're staring down significant pension and debt challenges. Like those rescuers poised outside the cave, we don't know exactly how we'll solve the issues in front of us, but we will. Don't be fearful. Instead, focus on the opportunities that will present. And no matter when you're reading this, or what the future holds—whether markets sit late cycle or early, richly priced or undervalued—know you have a dashboard of indicators that will help you gauge the market conditions and help you adapt.

While some are happy to do it all themselves, others need help and guidance to reach the goals they've set for themselves and their families. Ultra-wealthy families build teams of specialists that help their families develop and adhere to a guided investment plan and tap into a network of relationships to source and assess special investment opportunities. In this day and age you can do the same, building a team of expert professionals focused on you and your family's needs. This is exactly what my team provides the advisors

---

52   Erik Shatzker, "Stanley Druckenmiller Is Embracing Risk Again, Just 'Timidly,'" *Bloomberg*, December 18, 2019, https://www.bloomberg.com/news/articles/2019-12-18/stanley-druckenmiller-is-embracing-risk-again-just-timidly.

and families with whom we work. We provide multi-family office guidance and resources for wealthy individuals, and we work with hundreds of advisors providing a turnkey asset management platform (TAMP)-model portfolios, back office services, technology, trading, access to the CMG and Mauldin network, and our ability to source and research special investment opportunities.

You can learn more at cmgwealth.com, or email me directly at Blumenthal@cmgwealth.com. Together, we can help you put a disciplined Core and Explore investment process in place, think through complex planning and investment opportunities, and if appropriate, give you access to select Explore opportunities sourced through our network of relationships. Above all else, our goal is to help you achieve what matters most to you, and I'm confident that we can accomplish it together.

# IMPORTANT DISCLOSURE INFORMATION

**Investing involves risk. Past performance is no guarantee of future results.** Different types of investments involve varying degrees of risk. Therefore, it should not be assumed that future performance of any specific investment or investment strategy (including the investments and/or investment strategies recommended and/or undertaken by CMG Capital Management Group, Inc. (or any of its related entities, together "CMG") will be profitable, equal any historical performance level(s), be suitable for your portfolio or individual situation, or prove successful. **No portion of the content should be construed as an offer or solicitation for the purchase or sale of any security.** References to specific securities, investment programs, or funds are for illustrative purposes only and are not intended to be and should not be interpreted as recommendations to purchase or sell such securities.

Certain portions of the content may contain a discussion of, and/or provide access to, opinions and/or recommendations of CMG (and those of other investment and noninvestment professionals) as of a specific prior date. Due to various factors, including changing market conditions, such discussion may no longer be reflective of current rec-ommendations or opinions. Derivatives and options strategies are not suitable for every investor, may involve a high degree of risk, and may be appropriate investments only for sophisticated investors who are capable of understanding and assuming the risks involved. Moreover, you should not assume that any discussion or information contained herein serves as the receipt of, or as a substitute for, personalized invest-ment advice from CMG or the professional advisors of your choosing. To the extent that a reader has any questions regarding the applicability of any specific issue discussed above to his or her individual situation, he or she is encouraged to consult with the professional advisors of his or her choosing. CMG is neither a law firm nor a certified public accounting firm, and no portion of this content should be construed as legal or accounting advice.

This presentation does not discuss, directly or indirectly, the amount of the profits or losses, realized or unrealized, by any CMG client from any specific funds or securities. Please note: in the event that CMG references performance results for an actual CMG portfolio, the results are reported net of advisory fees and inclusive of dividends. The performance referenced is that as determined and/or provided directly by the referenced funds and/or publishers, have not been independently verified, and do not reflect the performance of any specific CMG client. CMG clients may have experienced materially different performance based upon various factors during the corre-sponding time periods.

Information herein has been obtained from sources believed to be reliable, but we do not warrant its accuracy. This document is a general communication and is provided for informational and/or educational purposes only. None of the content should be viewed as a suggestion that you take or refrain from taking any action nor as a recommendation for any specific investment product, strategy, or other such purpose.

Please note that there is a potential conflict of interest as a result of CMG's business relationship with a principal of Syntax, LLC. CMG may utilize exchange-traded funds ("ETFs") sponsored by Syntax, LLC, or one of its affiliates, such as Syntax Advisors, LLC, an SEC registered investment adviser. A principal of Syntax and advisor to the ETFs is also a minority owner of CMG. Because CMG's minority owner can earn compensation from the ETFs, CMG's use of the ETFs presents a conflict of interest. CMG does not receive any compensation from Syntax for utilizing the ETFs.

**Hypothetical Presentations**: To the extent that any portion of the content reflects hypothetical results that were achieved by means of the retroactive application of a back-tested model, such results have inherent limitations, including: (1) the model results do not reflect the results of actual trading using client assets but were achieved by means of the retroactive application of the referenced models, certain aspects of which may have been designed with the benefit of hindsight; (2) back-tested performance may not reflect the impact that any material market or economic factors might have had on the advisor's use of the model if the model had been used during the period to actually manage client assets; and (3) CMG's clients may have experienced investment results during the corresponding time periods that were materially different from those portrayed in the model.

Please also note: **past performance may not be indicative of future results**. Therefore, no current or prospective client should assume that future performance will be profitable or equal to any corresponding historical index (e.g., S&P 500® Total Return or Dow Jones Wilshire US 5000 Total Market Index). For example, the S&P 500® Total Return Index (the "S&P 500®") is a market capitalization-weighted index of five hundred widely held stocks often used as a proxy for the stock market. S&P Dow Jones chooses the member companies for the S&P 500® based on market size, liquidity, and industry group representation. Included are the common stocks of industrial, financial, utility, and transportation companies. The historical performance results of the S&P 500® (and those of all indices) and the model results do not reflect the deduction of transaction and custodial charges, nor the deduction of an investment management fee, the incurrence of which would have the effect of decreasing indicated historical performance results. For example, the deduction combined annual advisory and transaction fees of 1.00% over a ten-year period would decrease a 10% gross return to an 8.9 percent net return. The S&P 500® is not an index into which an investor can directly invest. The historical S&P 500® performance results (and those of all other indices) are provided exclusively for comparison purposes only, so as to provide general comparative information to assist an individual in determining whether the performance of a specific portfolio or model meets, or continues to meet, his or her investment objective(s). Corresponding descriptions of the other comparative indices are available from CMG upon request. It should not be assumed that any CMG holdings will correspond directly to any such comparative index. The model and indices performance results do not reflect the impact of taxes. CMG portfolios may be more or less volatile than the reflective indices and/or models.

In the event that there has been a change in an individual's investment objective or financial situation, he or she is encouraged to consult with his or her investment professional.

Written Disclosure Statement. CMG is an SEC-registered investment advisor located in Malvern, Pennsylvania. Stephen B. Blumenthal is CMG's founder and CEO. Please note: the above views are those of Stephen Blumenthal and do not reflect those of any subadvisor that CMG may engage to that may manage any CMG strategy. A copy of CMG's current written disclosure statement discussing advisory services and fees is available upon request or via CMG's internet web site at www.cmgwealth.com/disclosures.

# DISCLOSURES

The information provided is for educational purposes only. Past performance is no guarantee of future results.

For the Greenrock Model, the 10-Year Treasury, the Aggregate, and the S&P, "returns" shown are total rates of return compounded annually for periods greater than one year, with dividends and/or interest reinvested. As such, "returns" are a measure of gross performance and have not been adjusted to reflect management fees, custodial fees, or other expenses that are normally incurred in an actual client account.

Comparison of the Model to the S&P, the Aggregate and the 10-Year Treasury is subject to the material differences in the creation and representation of each, including the fact that the Model may contain asset classes and/or securities not included in the indices and therefore its performance relative to the indices will be impacted by this difference. Without limitation, the volatility of the indices will generally be different than that of the Model, which may affect the comparability of returns over specific time periods.

10-Year Treasury yield data is from the St. Louis Federal Reserve (FRED)

US Treasury Bellwether 10 Year total return from February 1981 – current provided by Morningstar Direct

10 Year Treasury total returns prior to February 1981 taken from Robert Schiller's Irrational Exuberance (2000).

Total returns for the Bloomberg Barclays US Aggregate Index provided by Morningstar Direct

Bloomberg Barclays US Aggregate Index statistics provided by Bloomberg

S&P 500 statistics provided by Bloomberg

Liquid Alternative Manager statistics provided by Bloomberg based on Greenrock monthly model performance

Historical data for returns on the S&P 500 provided by Morningstar Direct: January 1974 to current. Prior to 1974, the US Large Cap total return data series from Ibbotson Associates provided by Morningstar Direct.

Dividend Portfolio total returns 2000 – current is the Greenrock High & Growing Dividend Model. The returns on a hypothetical model portfolio (the "Greenrock Model") to the performance of the S&P 500 Index (the "S&P") and the Barclays Aggregate Bond Index (the "Aggregate"). The entire period, starting in January 1, 2000, is hypothetical performance based on actual returns for the period. Back-tested or hypothetical performance does not reflect trading in actual accounts and is intended for illustrative purposes only. The Model was constructed using the aggregation of the Model's underlying individual manager's historical monthly total returns weighted by the individual manager's appropriate model allocation, i.e. Monthly return = ((Mgr1 return * Mgr1 wt) + (Mgr2 return x Mgr2 wt) + ...), calculated monthly and rebalanced annually or when the model allocation changes. It is designed to reflect the investment objectives and strategies described in this brochure. The Model was constructed using the total returns from the separate account managers, mutual funds, and ETFs which we employ. Separate accounts generally have a minimum account size requirement. The Model portfolio results do not represent the results of actual trading and may not reflect the impact that material economic and market factors might have had on an adviser's decision-making if the adviser were actually managing a client account. In particular, the Model results do not necessarily reflect the application of each of the strategies described in this brochure. Clients whose portfolios were managed in whole or in part based on the strategies described may have investment results materially different from those portrayed in the Model. Dividend Portfolio total returns prior to 2000 provided by Jeremy Siegel, *Future for Investors* (2005).

# ACKNOWLEDGMENTS

A special thanks to Mark Finn, John Mauldin, Rory Riggs, John Ray, and Tom Giachetti for teaching me so much and—even more importantly—for the gift of friendship. My friends Kevin Malone, Dr. Lacy Hunt, David Kotok (and Camp Kotok friends), and David Rosenberg, I am grateful for your exceptional research and support in the debate over important and often confusing macroeconomic issues. Thank you to Ned Davis and the Ned Davis Research team for your invaluable work, and to the team at CMG whose excellence, support, and friendship made this book possible. PJ, Andrew, Linda, Avi, Todd, Magda, Adam, Brian, Mike, Rick, Mike, Keeley, and Stephanie, you truly make the journey wonderful. And a special thank you to Ariel Hubbard and the team at ForbesBooks. Professionalism at its finest.

# ABOUT THE AUTHOR

Steve Blumenthal started his career at Merrill Lynch in 1984, marking the beginning of his education on investor behavior and what it means for the markets. Shortly after, in 1987, he'd receive the greatest investing advice he'd ever encounter from the great Sir John Templeton: "The secret to my success is that I buy when everyone else is selling and I sell when everyone else is buying." With that advice in mind, he founded CMG Capital Management Group, Inc., in 1992. CMG specializes in tactical investments, with the ultimate goal of helping advisors and clients build portfolios focused on growth while mitigating downside risk.

Blumenthal shares the insights he has gained as a frequent speaker and writer on investment strategies. He is the author of the popular weekly e-letter On My Radar, which helps investors, advisors, and institutions achieve a deeper understanding of the forces driving the economy and investment markets. He also writes investment commentary for *Forbes* and has been featured in *The Wall Street Journal, Barron's, Investor's Business Daily, Pensions & Investments, Investment News,* and ETF.com. He has appeared on Bloomberg, CNBC, and Fox Business News, among other media outlets.

He graduated with a bachelor of science in accounting from Pennsylvania State University.

## OUR SERVICES

Founded in 1992, CMG Capital Management Group, Inc., is a registered investment advisor located in Malvern, Pennsylvania. CMG works with hundreds of independent investment advisors providing a best-in-class technology-driven turnkey asset management platform ("TAMP") solution. CMG's Private Client Group works with select families to provide multifamily office solutions and services. To learn more, email blumenthal@cmgwealth.com or call 610-989-9090 x140.